Routledge Revivals

I0127732

The Perversity of Politics

First published 1986, *The Perversity of Politics* talks about the perverse nature of political behaviour. Highly paradoxical, the seeking of advantage is of dual character, consisting not only in the spoils of conquest but in the rewards of co-operation. These two facets of politics pose the perennial question of why co-operation's inviting prospects have never yet immunized politics- domestic and international- against the perils and sacrifices of conflict.

The book finds an answer in the notion of the power overtone. Quest for security, more than immediate gratification, involves maneuver by individuals and groups for future freedom of action. The perversity of politics is heightened by sources of conflict that defy ultimate solution. Of ancient vintage is the uneasy relationship of attraction and repulsion between religion and state, each side uncertain as to where advantage lies. Nor is perversity dispelled by the social sciences, themselves caught in the dogmatics of nature versus nature, typified in the fundamentally different approaches to governance by James Madison and Karl Marx. Citing the American experience in particular the final chapter contends that democratic government is best designed to abate the power overtone and to mitigate conflict. This is a must read for students of political studies and political sociology.

The Perversity of Politics

Edward H. Buehrig

Routledge
Taylor & Francis Group

First published in 1986
by Croom Helm Ltd.

This edition first published in 2024 by Routledge
4 Park Square, Milton Park, Abingdon, Oxon, OX14 4RN

and by Routledge
605 Third Avenue, New York, NY 10017

Routledge is an imprint of the Taylor & Francis Group, an informa business

© 1986 Edward H. Buehrig

Publisher's Note
The publisher has gone to great lengths to ensure the quality of this reprint but points out that some imperfections in the original copies may be apparent.

Disclaimer
The publisher has made every effort to trace copyright holders and welcomes correspondence from those they have been unable to contact.

A Library of Congress record exists under ISBN: 0709932014

ISBN: 978-1-032-64359-5 (hbk)
ISBN: 978-1-032-64363-2 (ebk)
ISBN: 978-1-032-64362-5 (pbk)

Book DOI 10.4324/9781032643632

The Perversity of Politics

EDWARD H. BUEHRIG

CROOM HELM
London • Sydney • Dover, New Hampshire

© 1986 E. Buehrig
Croom Helm Ltd, Provident House, Burrell Row,
Beckenham, Kent BR3 1AT
Croom Helm Australia Pty Ltd, Suite 4, 6th Floor,
64-76 Kippax Street, Surry Hills, NSW 2010, Australia

British Library Cataloguing in Publication Data

Buehrig, E.
  The Nature of politics.
  1.Political science
  I. Title
  320'.01   JA74

  ISBN 0-7099-3201-4

Croom Helm, 51 Washington Street, Dover,
New Hampshire 03820, USA

Library of Congress in Publication Data applied for

Printed and bound in Great Britain by Mackays of Chatham Ltd, Kent

CONTENTS

To Margaret, a loyal companion

PREFACE

P.J. Vatikiotis and Peter Fraenkel, friends of long-standing, are largely responsible for the present undertaking. Beyond mere encouragement, their prodding was needed to overcome not inertia alone, but lack of certainty as to exactly what lesson the pursuit of political science for some fifty years had taught me.

Needless to say, acquiescence in the perversity of politics is not what attracted a youth — horror-struck by the First World War — to the study of political science. Actually, of course, governance everywhere struggles with recalcitrance, and nowhere does it escape the threat of palsy that the struggle portends. To this, unaided, any library can testify; but, in the event, I learned the lesson by experience as well. During the Second World War, service in the postwar planning division of the Department of State showed me the narrow confines within which policy is free to move, while, subsequently, residence in Lebanon and acquaintance with the Middle East in general revealed how exceptional the amenities of democracy are in dealing with the wild beast of politics. For the most part, politics in the Middle East — as elsewhere — defies institutional confinement. Contending with the dilemma of power produces diverse regimes — and differences too of subtle nuance — in response not to strategies common to a discipline of political science but to the endless peculiarities of historical circumstance.

Preface

I am much indebted to my colleagues York Willbern and Byrum Carter for their helpful reading of portions of the manuscript. For its typing, I greatly appreciate the patience and good humour of Barbara Hopkins. I need hardly add that what follows is a highly personal statement and that its depiction of politics is mine alone.

E.H.B.
Bloomington, Indiana.

INTRODUCTION

Central to man's nature and his history, political motivation pervades all of human relations, wherever wills mix — among individuals or among the many groupings into which individuals coalesce — and whatever the mixture, whether of conflict or cooperation.

Seeking advantage is of the essence, but politics is highly paradoxical; a dangerous game, to be sure, but also capable of yielding the fruits of mutual endeavour. Of dual character, advantage consists not only in the spoils of conquest but in the rewards of cooperation. Such are the two facets. They pose the perennial question of why cooperation's inviting prospects have never yet immunised politics — domestic and international — against the hazards of conflict.

The book's response to this query begins with the point made in Chapter 1 that politics, more than seeking immediate gratification, involves as well manoeuvre for future freedom of action. Such concern we have called the 'power overtone' — a term that some may regard as too weak a characterisation of so important an aspect of politics, but that has the merit of saying that manoeuvre for advantage does not preclude politics from performing its workaday function of satisfying mutual needs. To be sure — inescapably — the power overtone poses a choice between short- and long-term goals that entails not only

1

quandary but hazard: the dire risk of rendering a highly problematical future more dangerous still. It is slippery ground;
strategies are opposed as between adversaries, while within
each camp debate is further cause of division. Equating influence with power, Chapter 2 depicts the power overtone in its
many guises, ranging all the way from fighting effectiveness to
moral example.

Nor does this exhaust the discord to which politics is prone.
In still another dimension, the quest for security separates into
pursuits mundane and spiritual. Qualitatively different, yet they
intertwine in a relationship of repulsion and attraction, each
side uncertain as to where advantage lies. Chapter 3 treats the
patterns of rivalry threefold: alliance, separation, and hostility.
Authority's legitimising principle (God, people, proletariat)
varies with the pattern, and authority's allocation varies too,
internationally as it affects international law and domestically
as it affects human rights.

The title of Chapter 4, 'The Dogmatics of Conflict', reflects
the irony that conflicting theories about conflict are themselves
fertile cause of conflict. The nature of politics cannot but be a
prime concern of social science, yet, caught in the dichotomy of
nature versus nurture, intellectualised inquiry into the cause of
conflict is itself infected with the power overtone. Professional
aplomb among argumentative social scientists is not alone at
stake, so, too, are fundamental policy choices. The difference in
point of departure and prescription can be as great as that
between Karl Marx and James Madison: between the former's
confidence in a remade society and the latter's scepticism about
human nature.

How society for the most part stays afloat — despite the
hazards engrained in the very act itself of seeking security — is
the subject of Chapter 5. Means of survival, ranging on a continuum from cultivation of good manners to forceful domination, are in no two societies the same. Most telling, however, is

evolution of a legal system, a body of principles and procedures that protect society against members measuring their relations among themselves and with government in terms of power alone. A minority among states, mostly authoritarian, such politics are further imperilled by an international environment in which the power overtone runs rampant.

1 QUEST FOR SECURITY

The word 'politics' covers two very different kinds of behaviour. It encompasses the workings of government in pursuit of the general welfare, while it is equally applicable to the absence of mutual endeavour, even to the point of war. In short, it covers both cooperation and conflict.

Yet the accustomed usage of the word is singularly appropriate. Cooperation and conflict are antithetical, to be sure. However, both alike respond—neither less than the other—to friction in human relations. That a single word should cover the whole gamut of possible responses is not contradictory but symbiotic. Intimately linked, each of the opposing facets gains its character in association with the other. Without genesis in the challenge of conflict, cooperation would be undeserving of any credit for hard-won achievement—making an irrelevance of virtue itself. Contrariwise, if all were tension, if conflict were unrelieved, society could never have got a start. Politics in the first instance would dissolve in harmony, while in the second, the species itself would disappear owing to its incapacity for cooperation.

The mixture of cooperation and conflict varies widely among countries and across time. Granted that friction attracts the historian (as well as the journalist) more readily than harmony, one can still hardly question—least of all in the twentieth century—the widespread reality of conflict. Indeed, struggle for advantage may overwhelm all else; but politics is not always a pitiless game in which one player's gain is another's loss. It can confer mutual benefits, boons that are the very justification of authority. Admittedly, however, the use of authority is not necessarily and always cooperative. Mutuality is lacking when government is exploited for the benefit of a tyrant or a faction. Moreover, whether benign or malignant, government is not the only channel through which values are distributed, nor, by the same token, is authority the sole context in which politics occurs. In the domestic realm, the private sector (not excluding its criminal element) is busily engaged in determining who gets what, while in the international realm—with no presiding authority whatsoever—there is no lack of processes involved in the distribution of values.

The coexistence of cooperation and conflict is well illustrated by the course of international politics since the end of the Second World War. In sharp contrast to the inter-war period, these years have escaped economic collapse. Indeed, they have witnessed the manifold expansion of trade and finance across national lines. Growth of a global economy, and management of world-wide systems of transportation and communication, bespeak cooperation of a high order—private no less than public. These years have also escaped the political disaster of the earlier period. For forty years the world has been spared repetition of cataclysmic collapse such as twice overtook it in the preceding forty.

Absence of débâcle, economic and political, is the more remarkable when one turns to the conflictual side of politics since the Second World War. Civil and international wars—while they have not coalesced in world war—have exacted an appalling toll in terms of human life, political refugees, and destruction of property.

Taking the period 1945-75, an estimated 265 major conflicts occurred, domestic and international, including 94 coups and eight large-scale riots.[1] When one considers the toll taken by civil war in China, the Korean war, the almost continuous warfare in Indo-China, the war of independence in Algeria, and civil war in Nigeria, to cite but a few major convulsions, the number of people meeting violent death attributable to politics during the thirty years in question (and in subsequent years) undoubtedly exceeds the 15 million who died in battle during the Second World War. Indeed the number probably approaches the overall count—including civilians—of persons killed incident to warfare from 1939 until 1945.

The political refugee is another spin-off of politics. Little known in the nineteenth century, he is familiar in the twentieth on a scale without precedent. At first a European phenomenon beginning with the flight from the Bolshevist revolution, he continued to be European in the wake of the Second World War; vast numbers of displaced persons resisted repatriation to Eastern Europe. Soon, however, the political refugee became a tragic figure world-wide. Ideology continues to breed persecution, while increasing numbers of people have fallen victim to the ethnic incompatabilities of would-be nation states. In the Middle East, religions still refuse to mix, while British withdrawal from the Indian subcontinent precipitated fission of nuclear proportions between Hindu and Moslem. Cuba has generated a flood of refugees, as have Central America, Indo-China, Afghanistan, Iran, etc. The United Nations High Commissioner for Refugees recently estimated the number of political refugees to be of the order of 15 million. No continent has escaped: Africa, with its proliferation of new countries, least of all.

Compilations of persons killed or made homeless by politics are approximate at best. Still more so are calculations of the destruction of property. Clearly, however, rioting alone in the past forty years has destroyed property worth billions of dollars, while warfare accounts for many billions more.

Distribution of values—whether material or psychic—is what politics is all about. However, the characterisation of politics as arbiter errs on the side of cooperation as, conversely, its depiction as a scramble errs on the side of conflict. How, then, can politics be defined in such manner as to admit both cooperation and conflict into a single formula? How to reduce opposites to a common denominator? It can be done. Whatever the means— whether wisely or foolishly chosen—the end is the same. Simply put, politics is the quest for security—not just safety but, including freedom of action, security in the broadest sense.

The goal, of course, is elusive and the quest is ceaseless. To be sure, the decision-maker is not without guidelines. Legal norms are highly relevant. Policy may also look to the physical and natural sciences, if, for example, the question is one of health, or safety, or the environment. And, of course, the very rationale of the social sciences is to afford guidance in the affairs of society. However, guidelines are seldom definitive. Whether the normative injunctions of law or the demonstrable criteria of science, they operate within a penumbra of arguable application. There is no objectivity so pure as to overcome objections to the differential effects of a policy. Even those who gain are not easily satisfied, while those who lose are hard to reconcile. In short, the struggle for advantage persists; it cannot be suppressed. Caught in the middle, the policy-maker's is not an enviable role. But his dilemma—beyond the cupidity of his constituents—is of greater moment still.

Security is not a fixed target on which the policy-maker can take steady aim. How best to play his hand is a gamble. Risk is inescapable. Even with benefit of hindsight historians debate the wisdom of a policy's location on the continuum of passivity versus dynamism: whether exertion was unduly timid or overly bold. Error, whether of apathy or bellicosity, is fraught with serious, even dire, consequence. History is littered with the disasters of such misjudgement.

Timidity is not necessarily the mark of a status quo policy, nor need such a policy be disparaged as simply the path of least resistance. Its adoption may maximise security above any other choice; if the status quo is comfortable and free of threat, one is not inclined to tamper with it. But circumstances are seldom so indulgent. Typically the decision-maker, whether in regard to his own personal career, or on behalf of one or another of the numerous groupings into which individuals coalesce (family, church, university, business, nation, etc.), is in a quandary as to how far, if at all, he should move away from such shelter as the status quo affords. Of course, if the present is untenable, then to abandon it, however uncertain the future, would be the lesser evil. If, however, the status quo is not altogether intolerable, one cannot dismiss the cost of leaving it: the further one moves toward the dynamic end of the policy continuum the more one's flanks are exposed to attack.

Whether the risk is worth taking, and if so in what degree, are the imponderables of statesmanship. Typically, almost instinctively, the policy-maker fashions today's action with an eye to the future: how best to maximise tomorrow's safety and/or freedom of action. To that end, heavy sacrifice of present need, even of life itself, has been deemed over and over again to be a justifiable cost. Yet the future is conjectural at best. The cultivation of foresight—a challenge to all of social science and to political science in particular—is not to be discouraged; but at best policy cannot ensure a desired outcome. Indeed, the rudder's response to the helm is highly erratic.

The future harbours both peril and promise. The former inspires fear. Examples come to mind readily enough: the American forfending of communism in Indo-China, or the huge expenditure of governments on armaments. Indeed, so pervasive is fearful anticipation of the future as to obscure its opposite: the motivating force of hope. The promise of technology as perceived by business and government prompts large expenditure on the problematical outcome of research and development. The dubious investment of the British and French governments in supersonic flight comes to mind—as do notable instances of success, such as the Japanese gamble on the potentialities of technology.

The future beckons not merely in terms of material advantage. Not even mainly in such terms. Nor does fear alone induce the greater sacrifice. Ambition too—and hope—beckon and are inducements to the acceptance of risk. Nationalistic design readily flouts economic gain. So does the pursuit of justice; presumably the supreme guarantee of security, its achievement is a will-'o-the-wisp rendering the idealist highly vulnerable to the hazards of political endeavour. (Similarly the adventurer, for whom security is less a goal than a bore demanding the diversion of excitement.)

Anticipating the future is an integral part of decision-making. For its intended effect on tomorrow's safety and/or freedom of action, today's decision is different from what it otherwise would be. Here then is another guideline, one that readily takes precedence over short-run considerations of well-being. Motivation spurred on by anxiety, no less by ambition, or indeed by hope, is what is peculiarly political about politics. Equated here with all forms of influence—not just physical force—we shall call it the 'power overtone'.

Notes

1. William Eckhardt and Edward Azar, 'Major World Conflicts and Interventions, 1945–1975', *International Transactions*, vol. 5, no. 1 (1978).

2 THE POWER OVERTONE

Policy devoid of power occurs: but only if there is no opportunity for the cultivation of influence. Such lack is a rarity: a situation so desperately adverse as to thwart the well-practised wiles of the policy-maker, leaving no room for manoeuvre. But it has happened.

Ishi, a member of the Yahi Indian tribe, was in just such a strait. For many years his people, fleeing the white man, had retreated further and further into the harsh terrain of northern California. Attrition took its toll until finally Ishi was the lone survivor. Driven by privation and despair, he descended into the valley, where, one morning in August 1911, he was found in a corral, a huddled figure surrounded by yelping dogs. Ishi could hardly have acted from ulterior motives, not even from expectation of pity, a sentiment wholly unknown to the past enmity between Yahis and whites. Nor, needless to say, was the utter abjectness of the act tempered by awareness of the power of publicity. Actually, as news of a 'wild man' spread, Ishi became an object of curiosity. Having come to the attention of a University of California anthropologist, his unique value was quickly recognised and security came in the guise of a specimen. Even so, it cannot have been a wholly unwelcome fate; the attention it afforded was undoubtedly a source of satisfaction. Meanwhile, what of the past? Did Ishi regret the sacrifices of his dwindling people during the many years when they could have found not hostility, but succour, among the whites, whose dominance had become so overwhelming as to afford magnanimity? Or did he, instead, choose to romaniticise its deprivations as the self-imposed cost of a prideful independence? But whatever his ruminations, Ishi's act that August morning was born of such despair as to cast him down defenceless before his enemy.[1]

Of opposite nature, policy prompted by power alone is an occurrence rather more common. Indeed, the husbanding of influence can become an obsession.

For two months after the convening of the United States Congress in 1952, the Joint Committee on Atomic Energy was deadlocked. While pressing problems waited, its House and Senate members were in a tug of war over the chairmanship. The former insisted that the chair was their turn, while the Senators contended that it should always be theirs. Questions of substance played no part whatsoever in the dispute. Nor did partisanship between the Republican and Democratic parties enter into it. Neither were there any personal rivalries. It was strictly a fight between the House and the Senate over prestige and precedent. Appealing to principle, the Senators cited their constitutional responsibility to act on nominations and give advice and consent to treaties, while the Representatives pointed to their constitutional prerogative to initiate appropriations and taxes. It took a conference of the highest Congressional leaders to prescribe the obvious solution: that the chairs of all joint committees should rotate between House and Senate biennially.[2]

Heedless, yes, even ludicrous; yet such behaviour is not unfamiliar. Its inanities and hazards are known and deplored. War may eventuate, or—short of war—a debilitating arms race, and always the distortions of propaganda, demeaning to propagandist and victim alike. Yet the power overtone cannot be exorcised. Individuals and groups endeavour to store up a fund of influence both as buffer against adversity and as a reservoir on which to draw should fortune beckon. An asset in its own right, the allure of power is betrayed even by those who would negate it. Prudence itself entails risk.

How disputes are resolved (or at least defused) in the face of the power overtone is the subject of Chapter 5. Here we shall note instances of its presence in the arena of international politics, where there is no acknowledgement of a supreme authority and where—compared to domestic politics—the expectation of violence is close to the surface. For its part, of course, domestic politics takes on an international character when, as is not uncommon, crisis is too much for constitutional propriety to contain.

Prestige is of different kinds and quality. If regard for one's fellows is transparently sincere, its reward in esteem can be very great. Gandhi's saintliness was more powerful than the violence that he renounced. Exemplary, too, but less daunting in its demands, is honour's reward for uprightness. But, if saintliness can be tempted by fame, so manly reputation too has its vulnerable side.

It was honour in its unflattering guise that in 1968 figured in a flare-up between India and Sri Lanka. The island of Kachchativu lies between them in the Palk Strait. In area hardly more than a third of a square mile, consisting of sand and coral, it is uninhabited. When a banner headline in the Colombo papers announced that the 'Ceylon Government Takes Over Kachchativu', the Indian Parliament worked itself up to a fever pitch of indignation. Caught by surprise, the Foreign Ministry scurried for reference books to discover the location of the island and the spelling of its name. Speaking to the upper house, Mrs Indira Gandhi said that the two countries planned to hold talks and cautioned the deputies not to blow the dispute out of proportion, adding that the island 'doesn't even have drinking water'. Angry deputies rose from their benches in a chorus of protest, charging the Prime Minister with minimising the crisis and attempting to muzzle Parliament.[3]

Literally, the power overtone can attach itself to sticks and stones—in this instance to a tiny piece of real estate of no value whatsoever. Indeed, coincident with the Kachchativu affair, perversity was doubly underscored. As an aftermath of the India-Pakistani war of 1965, an arbitral tribunal announced its award of 317 square miles of desolate mud flats in the Rann of Kutch to Pakistan. The Indian Parliament was in a furore of righteous wrath, demanding that the award be rejected (which, however, the government refused to do).

Of course, however worthless economically, a barren piece of real estate may be invaluable (even measured in lives) from the standpoint of fighting effectiveness. Land and air transportation have in recent times reduced the strategic importance of such narrowing of the sea lanes as occurs at Gibraltar and the Dardanelles. At the same time, however, an importance, unprecedented, attaches to the Straits of Hormuz.

In the region of the Persian Gulf, history has brought a junction between its geological and human dimensions that could hardly be less propitious. Ages ago the convulsions of the earth's crust deposited an enormous pool of oil destined to be accessible around the coasts and under the waters of a cul-de-sac, where, moreover, traditional societies—fragmented by internecine rivalries—were one day to be caught in the toils of the twentieth century. Meanwhile, control of the Straits of Hormuz, through which scores of tankers pass to and fro, is cause of dissension locally and the preoccupation of military strategists worldwide.

As a factor affecting policy, expectation of violence results in a circular dilemma: scramble for advantage in terms of fighting effectiveness is itself a major cause of war. Such irony invites belief in explanations of conflict seemingly less captious than that afforded by the power overtone: for one thing, ascribing to one's enemy such menace as to justify the sacrifices of preparing against him, or, for another, choosing to discount the dynamics of the power overtone and settling instead on economic gain as the more tangible and, therefore, sufficient explanation of political behaviour. (Discovery of offshore oil occurred late in American involvement in Vietnam, news of which was greeted in some quarters as revealing at long last the real concern of American policy.)

Such recourse—politics as handmaiden to economics—is popular because of its simplicity. Of course, politics and economics are closely intertwined: essential to security is the accessability of resources. Indeed, the very foundation of an economy is itself a political construct. Take, for example, the international law governing propertyship over oil. As a resource indispensable to welfare, oil—like the mineral resources of the deep sea-bed—could be regarded as the inheritance of all mankind: though, as the legislative history of the Law of the Sea Treaty amply demonstrates, such a principle cannot itself settle critical questions about the structure and scope of the controlling authority. Actually, of course, the Western state system, based on authority territorially defined and confined among equals (however arbitrary the consequences), consigns propertyship in oil (however erratic its distribution) to the territorial sovereign—seaward, even, to a breadth of 200 miles. Making virtue out of cupidity, the juridical principle of territorial jurisdiction all the more firmly places resources in the willing grasp of an indigenous population, a grasp tightened further still by the ever increasing value in terms of fighting effectiveness that science and technology attach to the contents of the earth's crust.

Struggle between economic and political argument is aptly

illustrated by the great debate that erupted between the wars over American intervention in 1917.[4] An epic example of the clash between economic and political perspectives, the controversy, more than academic, paralysed American foreign policy for two decades. Host to the power overtone, historiography's depiction of the past was made to serve the politics of the present. Munitions makers and bankers were charged by the isolationists with hucksterism for their own gain, an allegation whose popularity was difficult for the internationalists to overcome, while the Wilsonianism of the latter had a willfulness of its own. Actually, American entry into the First World War resulted from compulsions both economic and political, though mainly the latter.

Wilson's neutrality proclamation of August 1914 voiced the abstention from European politics that had long since become a fixed principle of American policy. Yet in 1917 this stance, initially uncontested, was abandoned. What, then, led to intervention? Had a reassessment of America's future security intervened, or was the declaration of war owing merely to transitory vicissitude on the oceanic highways?

As recently as 1907 the law of neutrality had reached its peak in the Hague Conventions; but this triumph of American diplomacy was short-lived. Subject at best to encroachment from the belligerents, neutral rights were vulnerable as well to the unforeseen changes in warfare wrought by science and technology. When war came, Great Britain immediately expanded the category of absolute contraband, and soon, having established a distant patrol—not a blockade—in the North Sea, the British confiscated American cargoes with Scandinavian, not just German, destinations. All of this was against the traditional rules. American protests were models of legal argument, but Britain was never pressed to a showdown.

The upshot was a striking contrast. On the one hand, German-American trade declined to an insignificant trickle, while, on the other, American trade with the Allies flourished. Thus American neutrality was without economic value to Germany, while American resources, agricultural and industrial, contributed immensely to the Allied war effort. One is tempted to say that in effect the German submarine was seeking to redress the balance and that taking issue with it was the price the United States paid for a highly profitable trade of one-sided advantage to the Allies. But such a reading would slight the ultimate political purpose of submarine warfare, while at the same time overemphasising American solicitude for trade.

The underlying cause of this discrepancy was British control over the sea lanes. It was this control that Germany was ambitious to overthrow and, with its own navy, to supplant. Unlike Germany, the United States was not hostile to British sea power—and not merely from a willingness to suffer British arrogance as the price of wartime prosperity. The strong American bias favouring Great Britain had roots in the kinship of their political institutions and, geopolitically, in parallel policies toward Latin America. In the absence through the greater part of the nineteenth century of a standing American navy—in spite of the proclamation of the Monroe Doctrine—British control of the Atlantic was a welcome shield to the Western Hemisphere. Also—illustrative of growing accommodation—by 1914 Anglo-American arbitrations had set a record in number and in intrinsic importance. Thus circumstances (unlike those leading to the future break with Japan) did not demand the prying apart of economic and political factors to determine their relative weight; a profitable wartime trade was consonant with the nineteenth century's legacy of Anglo-American accommodation. Protesting the while, but never to the sticking point, the United States permitted British sea power to work its inexorable effects—however conducive to dispute the unheralded concurrence of economic gain and political purpose would one day prove to be.

Meanwhile, the ambiguities of the law of neutrality—further confused by new weaponry and the pressures of total war—afforded fertile ground for the power overtone to take hold in unexpected ways. Under the traditional law, merchantmen were allowed to arm defensively against enemy commerce raiders. As against cruisers, such armament posed no threat of destruction; as against so frail a craft as the submarine, however, it was lethal. The upshot was that Great Britain used the illegalities of the submarine to justify shelling and ramming it on sight, while Germany used the illegalities of the merchantman to justify torpedoing it without warning. Caught in this vicious circle by virtue of neutral ports being restricted in their harbouring of war vessels, the United States was in a quandary. Yet, however much exasperated by British practices, Washington refrained from closing its ports to the armed merchantman, nor did it take the less drastic action of putting the armed merchantman off limits to American travel. Wilson's strong opposition to doing so affords an altogether unique example of the power overtone.

Up to 1 February 1917, when Germany launched unrestricted submarine warfare, only about ten American vessels had been assaulted. Three lives were lost. In all instances, Germany acknowledged responsibility. In other words, the recurring crises with Germany were over the death and injury of American passengers and crewmen on Allied, not American, merchantmen. This circumstance did not go unnoticed. In February 1916, Congressional leaders informed the President of overwhelming sentiment in Congress for prohibiting American passage on armed belligerent merchantmen. This challenge to his diplomacy was countered by Wilson in a remarkable letter of 24 February 1916 to Senator William Stone, Chairman of the Foreign Relations Committee:

For my own part, I cannot consent to any abridgement of the rights of American citizens in any respect. The honor and self-respect of the nation is involved. We covet peace, and shall preserve it at any cost but the loss of honor. To forbid our people to exercise their rights for fear we might be called upon to vindicate them would be a deep humiliation indeed. It would be an implicit, all but an explicit, acquiescence in the violation of the rights of mankind everywhere and of whatever nation or allegiance. It would be a deliberate abdiction of our hitherto proud position as spokesmen even amidst the turmoil of war for the law and the right. It would make everything this Government has attempted and everything that it has achieved during this terrible struggle of nations meaningless and futile.

It is important to reflect that if in this instance we allowed expediency to take the place of principle, the door would inevitably be opened to still further concessions. Once accept a single abatement of right and many other humiliations would certainly follow, and the whole fine fabric of international law might crumble under our hands piece by piece. What we are contending for in this matter is of the very essence of the things that have made America a sovereign nation. She cannot yield them without conceding her own impotency as a nation and making virtual surrender of her indepdent position among the nations of the world.

Clearly, entanglement with the armed merchantman could have been easily side-stepped. However, the Senate backed down. The power overtone — Wilson's coveting of an American reputation for the vindication of law — won out.

This as of February 1916. Highly ironical, therefore, is Wilson's weakened belief in the freedom of the seas issue a year later, even after the German government had for the first time declared neutral commerce to be an avowed target for destruction. By then he had begun to doubt the viability of the traditional law and, in any event, was finally disabused of the rules of maritime warfare as the measure of America's relation to Europe at war. After all, so shaky a foundation, narrowly concerned with trade in highly exceptional circumstances, could not but stultify a policy that admitted the dire possibility of going to war. Yet, Wilson was trapped. The diplomatic record — built on freedom of the seas, or, better, that modicum of freedom vouchsafed the neutral — could not in the end be disavowed. Trigger to war, it forms the initial theme of the War Address. The remainder of the Address, however, is of a different order. Midway, one can almost hear Wilson shifting gears as he moves finally to adumbration of a league of nations — to security embedded in law, but a regime very different indeed from that of the sea in wartime.

Ambition of a material sort is not to be found in the War Address. 'We desire no conquest, no dominion', Wilson said. Nor did America seek 'compensation for the sacrifices that we shall freely make'. There was, however, a note of fear—though not the elemental fear of military domination. In the presence of the 'organized power' of German autocracy, there could be 'no assured security for the democratic Governments of the world'.

But the future depended on more than defeat of Germany. America, Wilson said, would be fighting for 'the ultimate peace of the world and for the liberation of its peoples, the German peoples included; for the rights of nations great and small and the privilege of men everywhere to choose their way of life and of obedience. The world must be made safe for democracy.' Indeed, America's purpose was 'to set up amongst the really free and self-governed peoples of the world . . . a concert of purpose and of action . . .' This theme, that of a league of nations, was reiterated in the peroration: 'a universal dominion of right by such a concert of free peoples as shall bring peace and safety to all nations and make the world itself at last free.'

Not all voices were in harmony with Wilson's lawyer's outlook. William Jennings Bryan argued that a league to enforce peace would substitute physical force for moral influence, which would be a 'step down' from what America had always stood for. 'The idea is vital and controls destiny.' If America were to rely on moral example, 'it not only would not be attacked . . . , but it would become the supreme power in the world.' Theodore Roosevelt, on the other hand, had an instinctive feeling for balance of power in terms of fighting effectiveness. Robert Lansing, Wilson's Secretary of State after Bryan's resignation in the summer of 1915, contended that democratic societies — deemed to be pacific by nature — were a sufficient promise of peace in themselves; accordingly, he believed that the United States should join the Allies against Germany — without regard to the twists and turns of the submarine issue, and apart from any thought of a league of nations. Devotion to democracy was, of course, shared by Wilson, Bryan, and Roosevelt; but it remained for Lansing to cast the power overtone exclusively in the guise of ideology.

Readiness to pit the present against the future propelled the United States into war. Promise of tomorrow's security was deemed justification for today's sacrifice. Nor can one regard Bryan as evasive of such cost; on the contrary, his pacifism paid the considerable price of defying those who would, in his view, surrender to mere circumstance. The latter, for their part — even if at odds among themselves accepted participation in the war as an inescapable cost of future security.

From the beginning Roosevelt and Lansing scorned Wilson's preference for 'peace without victory'. In the end, however, Wilson too sought victory, but for honour's sake less so than Roosevelt and, unlike Roosevelt, not at all in terms of a future cast in the rigors of a balance of power. While more attuned to Lansing's belief in democracy, Wilson's was in addition an overarching conception of a new future based on international law and organisation. Such was the hope — neither ambition nor fear, but hope — that emerged as the supreme justification for risking American entry into war. But the war had already weakened the foundations of Western Civilisation. Not the future envisioned by Wilson (nor, indeed, that predicted by Lenin), but a Hitler and a Stalin were to be the fruit of a mindless struggle for power.

Notes

1. W. H. Hutchinson, 'Ishi — the Unconquered', *Natural History* (March 1949), pp. 126—33.
2. *New York Times*, 5 April 1953.
3. *New York Times*, 5 March 1968.
4. Edward H. Buehrig, *Woodrow Wilson and the Balance of Power* (Bloomington: Indiana University Press, 1955); see especially Chapter 4, 'Defense of Trade' and Chapter 5, 'Defense of Principle'.

3 RELIGION AND STATE

Even in favourable circumstances, security is elusive. Between seeker and sought, power in its many permutations is an ever present challenge to rectitude and to prudence, posing hazard for timid and bold alike. More than just immediate gratification, security entails as well the quandary of power.

Nor is that all. Security has still another dimension. The quest bifurcates into qualitatively different goals. Security, yes; but in the very different meanings of mundane and spiritual. The former quest pertains to society's workaday abrasions, whereas the latter concerns the human odyssey: the mystery of improbable creatures in an improbable universe. Prompted by cosmic anxiety — beyond the power of reason to dispel — the spiritual quest affirms the biblical truth that man lives not by bread alone.

Typically, the quests are institutionally differentiated, but, separate or not, they jostle over possession of common ground. Jealous rivalry is, of course, to be expected. However, more than superficial, tension runs deep. Religion prescribes man's conduct both in relation to God and his own kind, which then poses a question of obligation, whether it is incumbent on the State to enforce prescriptions and prohibitions deemed essential to salvation. In its turn, secular authority cannot but be tempted by the legitimisation that is within the power of religion to bestow. Needless to say the relationship is an uneasy one of attraction and repulsion, each side uncertain as to where advantage lies, whether in alliance, separation or hostility. Alliance has been unquestioned through the greater part of history. All the more novel, therefore, is the separation envisaged by the American constitution. Hostility, meanwhile, is exemplified by the harassment by communism of traditional religion: though, ironically, viewing the world through its own ideological prism, communism, itself tantamount to a religion, comes full circle. Central to all three patterns is the question of the nature and location of authority. No two answers are alike: God in the first instance, people in the second, and proletariat in the third.

So pervasive is man's preoccupation with the design and meaning of his existence that religion has given its name to whole civilisations, severing the Mediterranean world into Christian and Islamic and the Christian into Western and Eastern. Characteristic of religious belief is its kinship with authority — an intimacy that in fact constitutes the historical norm. Typically, orthodoxy anoints authority with divine sanction. But not without strings. Neither acquiescent nor gratuitous, the act, if not all-embracing in religion's favour, at least lays claim to partnership with the State. Yet, whatever the combination of secular and spiritual, enhanced harmony through alliance is a promise that history has seldom fulfilled.

Authority deriving from God presents the State with a conundrum. Jealous regard for singularity is in the nature of religion. In keeping with the emotional needs of the believer, stilling of cosmic anxiety requires both suppression of doubt and evangelistic zeal. Thus burdened, the State pays a heavy price for such benefit as may redound from religion's endorsement. The cost is both external to a polity and internal. Concession to unbelief in either direction incurs the charge of faithlessness. Internally, the State's treatment of rival beliefs raises the question of human rights, while externally the question is one of international law. The parameters for dealing with the first question are fixed — in answer to the second — by the manner of authority's allocation in the world at large.

Truth about man and his destiny cannot be circumscribed, neither in time nor space. Thus, differing world views, each claiming rightful supremacy and prophesying ultimate dominion, invite enmity. Their presumption of universality cannot escape the clash of authorities differently ordained. The centuries-old hostility between Christianity and Islam is a prime example.

A system of law deemed to be divine and comprehensive is the very essence of Islam. Obedience to religion's injunctions is coterminous with the whole of life. On what terms, then, can a society so conceived — a seamless web, as it were, spun by the jurist-theologian — relate to the outside world? Not surprisingly, a polity as highly juridical as the Islamic answers this question quite explicitly. Two worlds are posited, qualitatively different and of unequal status, Islamic and non-Islamic, the former designated *dar al-islam*, the latter *dar al-harb*. Islam means to submit — to the will of God — thus the first designation may be read as the 'house of peace', the second translates literally as the 'house of war'. Meanwhile, jihad is the doctrine of just, or holy, war. To be sure, warfare is not decreed as incessant. Actually, as we shall see, the status accorded 'people of the Book' is suggestive of human rights — going about as far in that direction as a religion-based polity can be made to stretch. Yet, if circumstances conspire, force against non-Muslims (or the heretic) is regarded as lawful and just.

Crusade — as regards both infidel and heretic — is the well-known Christian counterpart of jihad. As warfare carried on under Papal decree, it sanctioned the West's repeated attempts in the eleventh century and after to 'liberate' the Holy Land. While canon law seems never to have equalled Islamic sophistication in defining relations between faiths mutual only in that each excludes the other, there was nothing equivocal about Catholicism's claim to supreme authority world-wide based on God's deputation through His Son Jesus Christ. It was from the Pope that the Spanish rulers sought title to the Columbian discoveries. In Bull *Inter Caetera* of 3 May 1493, the Pope (the infamous Alexander VI) noted that:

> Among other works well pleasing to the Divine Majesty and cherished of our heart, this assuredly ranks highest, that in our times especially the Catholic faith and the Christian religion be exalted and everywhere increased and spread, that the health of souls be cared for and that barbarous nations be overthrown and brought to the faith itself.

The Pope then proceeded to

> give, grant, and assign forever to you and your heirs and successors, kings of Castile and Leon, all and singular the aforesaid countries and islands ... hitherto discovered ... and to be discovered ... together with all their dominions, cities, camps, places, and villages, and all rights, jurisdictions, and appurtenances of the same.[1]

The amplitude of the Papal gift is the greater when one remembers that Columbus confidently believed that he had indeed reached India and China.

China — whose true whereabouts were soon to be revealed — turned out to have a world view of its own, long-standing and deeply ingrained. Like Islam and Christianity, China too claimed universal supremacy. Absent, however, was justification in terms of religion. Neither buttressed nor challenged thus, authority was rooted in the Confucian ethic. Without supernatural help (the Mandate of Heaven lent but fickle support to successive dynasties), the underlying force of ethnocentricity was enough in itself to ascribe supremacy to the Dragon Throne. For centuries the Emperor claimed suzerainty over neighbouring rulers, entailing the rendering of tribute by them and the seeking of investiture on the occasion of a new accession. Nor was vassalage necessarily demeaning but regarded rather — such was the prestige of Chinese culture and civilisation — as part of the natural order of things. Thus, in contrast to the hortatory stance of Christianity and Islam, China — awe-inspiring to the West too at the outset — stood aloof in expectation of the outsider's deference. But, however fixed in its ancient habits, China could not finally withstand the inroads of science and of Western ideas about human rights. Presumption of a world ordered in accordance with Confucian norms was challenged no less traumatically than was Christian and Muslim dependence on revelation. Radical change was inevitable. Yet, unlike Japan's rapid adjustment to Commodore Perry's appearance in Yokohama Bay in 1853, China's reaction to the importunities of the West was grudging and obstinate. Lord Macartney was caught in the incompatabilities between East and West when in 1793 his mission to the Chinese court ended in fiasco. Sent by George III of England, Macartney's object was to establish diplomatic relations. More particularly, his purpose was amelioration of the vexations surrounding trade at Canton, conditions shaped by a mental set radically different from that underlying the market-place of the West. Denigrated in the Confucian scale of values, conduct of commerce, like all of Chinese society, was moulded by the all-pervasiveness of hierarchial thought.

In a Sinocentric world, the concept of diplomatic equality was unknown and in Macartney's time a Ministry of Foreign Affairs did not exist. Not until 1861 did China so adapt to the newly-learned norms of international law. At the outset of the century the ancient forms and ceremonies, placing the Imperial Court at the apex of the world order were still beyond question. Accordingly Macartney's was treated as a tribute-bearing mission. To be sure, the kowtow (abject prostration before the throne) was waived, in lieu of bended knee only. But no other concession was forthcoming. All requests were refused, refusal taking the form of a mandate, as was appropriate in response to what Chinese protocol regarded as a petition. The Emperor concluded by addressing King George thus:

> Swaying the wide world, I have but one aim in view, namely, to maintain a perfect governance and to fulfil the duties of the State: strange and costly objects do not interest me. If I have commanded that the tribute offerings sent by you, O King, are to be accepted, this was solely in consideration for the spirit which prompted you to dispatch them from afar. Our dynasty's majestic virtue has penetrated unto every country under Heaven, and Kings of all nations have offered their costly tribute by land and sea. As your Ambassador can see for himself, we possess all things. I set no value on objects strange or ingenious, and have no use for your country's manufactures. This then is my answer to your request to appoint a representative at my Court, a request contrary to our dynastic usage, which would only result in inconvenience to yourself. I have expounded my wishes in detail and have commanded your tribute Envoys to leave in peace on their homeward journey. It behoves you, O King, to respect my sentiments and to display even greater devotion and loyalty in future, so that, by perpetual submission to our Throne, you may secure peace and prosperity for your country hereafter. Besides making gifts (of which I enclose an inventory) to each member of your Mission, I confer upon you, O King, valuable presents in excess of the number usually bestowed on such occasions, including silks and curios — a list of which is like-

wise enclosed. Do you reverently receive them and take note
of my tender goodwill towards you! A special mandate.[2]

Always theoretically incompatible, universalisms, whether
Islamic, Christian, or Chinese, became practically so when discovery — joined by philosophy — exposed their ethnocentrism.
Global interaction, political and economic, was more than any
legacy out of the past could encompass or withstand. Legitimisation of authority and its allocation could no longer pander to
ideological fantasy. The upshot was transition to a pattern of
authority below the pretension of universal rule. International
law — newly conceived — lodged sovereignty in territorial units
and prescribed legal equality among them. Thus personal jurisdiction natural to a community of believers — as in Islam and
Christianity — gave way to territorial jurisdiction divided
among independent entities. Further still, authority — no
longer sanctified from above — came to rest on consent from
below.

Such, at any rate — territorial fragmentation of secularised
authority — is the rationale that underlies today's political map.
Appearances, however, can be deceptive. We shall note that
fundamentalism flouts territorial secularism and that communism constitutes still another ideological challenge to
international law. However, curiosity turns first to the origins of
a pattern of authority — unique to modern history — that
neglects religious sanction and forgoes universal dominion.

Coexistence, though it may be endured as a lesser evil, never
rates as an ideal. In medieval Europe the Jew was stigmatised
and the heretic anathematised. Yet the eighteenth century saw
the West turning pragmatic. By then, in Europe, authority had
precipitated into territorial units independent and equal. That
such should have originated in the West and not elsewhere is
owing to history's having forced an introspection that Europe
could not escape.

China, by contrast, was not similarly impelled to self-examination. A civilisation prodded not from within but from without contained small prospect for adapting authority to the existence of one world, not in fantasy, but in actual fact. Unabashed, China's ethnocentrism was still intact when the Emperor condescendingly refused King George's wish to establish a legation in Peking:

> Supposing that your Envoy should come to our Court, his language and national dress differ from that of our people, and there would be no place in which to bestow him. It may be suggested that he might imitate the Europeans permanently resident in Peking and adopt the dress and customs of China, but it has never been our dynasty's wish to force people to do things unseemly and inconvenient.

In the same vein, the Emperor continued:

> If you assert that your reverence for Our Celestial dynasty fills you with a desire to acquire our civilisation, our ceremonies and code of laws differ so completely from your own that, even if your Envoy were able to acquire the rudiment of our civilisation, you could not possibly transplant our manners and customs to your alien soil. Therefore, however adept the Envoy might become, nothing would be gained thereby.[3]

Similarly self-centred, but not wholly so, Islam accommodated diversity within limits. As best exemplified in the Ottoman Empire, Christians and Jews were exempt from the strict logic of their unbelief. True, they were not emancipated as individuals. In no sense did their treatment anticipate the tolerant scepticism of a Western liberalism that would one day proclaim freedom of religion as a fundamental human right. To be sure, among believers, equality is fundamental to Islam, but as between Muslim and non-Muslim identity and standing turn not on the individual but on his religion. Granting as much, the corporate status accorded to Christians and Jews under the millet system (the Arabic root *millah* ambiguously translates as religious community, people, or nation) is still a significant concession to diversity. Mohammed seen as culminating prophet in a line from Abraham through Jesus, means that, as forerunners to Islam, Jews and Christians are 'people of the Book'. Treated as autonomous communities, each was organised under its own ecclesiastical hierarchy; each had its own religion-based laws and courts; and each provided its own needs such as education and welfare. A head tax was owing; but there was no military obligation. Needless to say, conversion to Islam was encouraged, not to say pressed. The reverse, however, was not permitted; among Muslims proselytising was forbidden and apostasy subject to capital punishment. In this manner, for some 500 years, the potential for trouble was minimised in a population differentiated by religion. But not without cost. The Ottoman Empire was not conducive to a mobilised and progressive society.

Neither pattern of authority, Chinese or Islamic, was a likely prelude to the looming future. Both were anachronisms incapable of purging themselves of universalistic pretention. Reluctantly and spasmodically, in appearance if not in substance, both bowed to international law's injunction of authority territorially confined among equals. It does not follow, however, that international law was the product of futuristic thinking. Born not of foresight, the new order evolved blindly out of the cross-currents of European politics. Yet place of origin was not due to chance alone. Unknowingly, Christendom in its Western (not its Eastern) manifestation was favourable to the evolution of its namesake: the Western state system.

The course of history is a mixture of turbulence and logic. Tossed on a rough sea, it responds to the helmsman erratically at best. Stormy indeed, the European sea was vastly disturbed by the Renaissance. Consequences ricocheted unpredictably, and still do today, even in the West, not to speak of the devastating effect with which science and technology continue to work their way through the traditional societies of the non-Western world. To be sure, rationalism — the cutting edge of the revival of classicism — had consequences intellectually conceived and purposefully executed. Thus philosophy laughed divine right out of court. But religion was not easily deposed; not until the end of the eighteenth century did secular authority triumph. Meanwhile, already in the age of monarchy — long before the American and French revolutions—territorial rule had emerged; still attached, however, to divine right of kings. Presumption was that of a tolerant deity, one resigned to the fragmentation of his authority here below. So unlikely a scheme can hardly be regarded as the handiwork of theorists in recognition of an outmoded past. True, authors like Bodin (1530-96) and Grotius (1583-1645), though still writing very much in the medieval idiom, gave the new order an underpinning of political theory and juridical definition. Theirs was no blueprint, however, but essentially the rationalisation of a process already going on. Responding to the ferment of the Renaissance, political thought — unlike the new astronomy — was not the unaided work of sceptical scientific inquiry. Indeed, popular sovereignty as doctrinal alternative to divine right is not without theoretical and practical difficulties of its own.

The Renaissance was not alone in producing a new order. There was the powerful force of the Reformation, as well. However, prior to Renaissance and Reformation alike, and germane to the origins and effects of both, was long-standing and vigorous debate in Western Europe over the nature and location of authority.

The presence of this legacy is apparent in the thought of Franciscus de Vitoria (1480-1546), a Spaniard and Dominican, professor of theology and law at the University of Salamanca. Discoursing on the Indians newly discovered, he concluded that the Spanish rulers did not have rightful dominion over them, the Bull of 3 May 1493 to the contrary notwithstanding. Weighing — no less than his opponents — the authority of the Bible, the Christian Fathers, Aquinas, other theologians and Aristotle, Vitoria concluded that the 'Emperor is not the lord of the whole world'. He then turned to the question of the Pope:

> A second alleged title of the lawful possession of these lands and one that is vehemently asserted, is traced through the Supreme Pontiff. For it is claimed that the Pope is temporal monarch, too, over all the world and that he could consequently make the Kings of Spain sovereign over the aborigines in question, and that so it has been done.[4]

Disagreeing with this proposition and finding passages in the Bible disclaiming temporal power in Christ's name, Vitoria concluded that 'much less has the Pope it, he being Christ's vicar'. Yet, Vitoria concedes:

> The Pope has temporal power ... so far as it is in the subservience to matters spiritual ... Inasmuch ... as the Pope is a spiritual pastor by Christ's commission and the duties of this office can not be hindered by the civil power ... it is beyond doubt that power over things temporal has also been left to him so far as necessary for the government of things spiritual.

Vitoria grants that 'our Lord said that there should be "one flock and one shepherd" at the end of the age', but he finds in this 'sufficient proof that at the present day all are not sheep of this flock'. As he emphatically states: 'The Pope has no temporal power over the Indian aborigines or over other unbelievers ... For he has no temporal power save such as subserves spiritual matters. But he has no spiritual power over them ... Therefore he has no temporal power either.' Vitoria adds that

> even if the barbarians refuse to accept Christ as their lord, this does not justify making war on them or doing them any harm ... [I]t is utterly absurd for our opponents to say that, instead of the barbarians going scatheless for rejecting Christ, they should be bound to accept His vicar under penalty of war and confiscation of their property, aye, and penal chastisement.

As it turned out, the future eluded both sides in this debate. At home in Europe, Pope and Emperor were rapidly losing power to the nation-state. Also thwarted — again by the nation-state — was the Vitorian viewpoint. In his own time, newly forming nation-states had already begun to compete for dominion over the non-Western world. Prescient, to be sure, but Vitoria and others like him were of little weight against the ever-growing imbalance in the world owing to European technology. They were swept aside by the rush of ambition to which the imbalance gave licence. In asserting that discovery 'gives no support to a seizure of the aborigines any more than if it had been they who had discovered us', Vitoria's triumph over a purely European outlook, while it bespoke moral principle, disregarded political reality. That discovery should give title to territory comports with a power differential too great for international law to have gainsaid. Yet, ironically, over 400 years after Vitoria's lectures, the tables have turned. Today's countenancing of the proliferation of some 200 sovereign states shifts advantage away from Europe to the non-Western world. Non-discriminating as to societal background and permissive even as regards such essentials of efficacy as size of population and territory, international law is profligate of the unique privileges of statehood: not least juridical equality among its kind. The doctrine of equality affords leverage that the small state is loath to acknowledge and that common opinion fails fully to comprehend. One has but to recall Panama's success in wresting control of the Canal away from the United States.

As already stated, Vitoria's sophistication was not without precedent. If he was niggardly regarding the Pope, conceding only that modicum of secular authority 'necessary for the governance of things spiritual', Marsilio of Padua (c.1280-c.1343) had gone further still. Two hundred years before Vitoria, he flatly opposed papal supremacy, such as that claimed by Boniface VIII (Bull *Unam sanctum*, 1302), who saw Church and State as one with all authority vested in the Pope as vicar of Christ. Siding with Emperor against Rome, holding civil society to be self-sufficing and in no need of sanctification, Marsilio confined religious concern to the hereafter, while on earth — in a formula even less generous to the Pope than Vitoria's — he subordinated all moral and religious questions to secular control. Thus, when differentiating between authority spiritual and temporal, Marsilio gave voice to a distinction deeply rooted in the political culture of Western civilisation, a distinction reiterated many times over, before and after. The drama of Western Europe, as in no other history, is the story of secular authority pitted against spiritual. Yet, such was the strength of the latter that the Emperor was loath to forgo divine sanction — as were the latter-day monarchs. Complications with a Rome both spurned and beseeched prompted search for helpful distinctions between kinds of authority. Indeed, the search still goes on. If today the Supreme Court of the United States puzzles over a separation between Church and State, all the more comprehensible are Europe's wars over what is God's and what is Caesar's.

Amalgamation of Christendom into a seamless web in the manner of Islam, however appealing to Papal ambition, was precluded by historical circumstance. Whereas Islam established its own empire, Christendom inherited an empire. The great Roman tradition, having escaped the Church's full embrace, never ceased to thwart the latter's claim over the whole of society. It behoved medieval philosophy, therefore, to distinguish, as best it could, between governance and salvation, even if doing so gave countenance to rupture at the very heart of the body politic. However, so to differentiate between kinds of security, separately pursued, was not without compensating advantage. To accept hiatus and to abide clash between absolute and pragmatic, is the very prerequisite to political liberty. An anomaly to be sure: that a matter of such moment should rest on the uncertainties of scepticism rather than the imperatives of belief. Yet tolerance is born of the former, not the latter, and tolerance, in turn, is essential to freedom of thought and expression. Such, then, was the legacy of Medieval Europe. The theory of the two swords — neither subject to but each wary of the other — contained the seeds in domestic politics of human rights, and in international politics of territorial rule.

However much the Renaissance gave impetus in European thought to different kinds of security, secularism's greater gain was owing to schism. Theologically, Protestantism challenged the practice of a mechanistic salvation, while politically too — in a culture as strongly religious in orientation as the European — the Reformation was bound to have far-reaching repercussions. The effect was enhancement of the nation-state: internationally to delineate more sharply its independence and domestically to intensify its secularisation.

Only toleration could rescue Christendom from the bloody strife of contending beliefs, a toleration that, for one thing, favoured territorial rule as conducive to coexistence. Such was the formula in the Peace of Augsburg (1555). In each territory of the Empire the prince's choice as between Catholicism and Lutheranism became obligatory for his subjects: an adherent of the losing side being free to sell his property and to migrate. Such too — pacification of religious differences — was the back of Bodin's championing of sovereign independence in his work, *Six Livres de la République*, published in 1576. But, before toleration finally prevailed, Europe had yet to endure the religiously embittered wars, civil and foreign, of the seventeenth century. Only by the eighteenth century did the storm subside. Passionless and in singular contrast, its wars — not yet nationalistic — were dynastic in aim.

Domestically, where religious diversity was at its most divisive and geographical separation of no help, toleration was long in coming, and even then (with the exception of the American Constitution) not as equality between faiths but as forbearance by an established church toward its rivals. English history affords a prime example of just how long and in what manner. Taking full charge of his realm, Henry VIII's assumption of ecclesiastical authority (Act of Supremacy, 1534) etched a territorial independence of immediate and lasting effect; through abolition of the Church's jurisdictional prerogatives and expropriation of its vast landed properties, statehood was conferred on a burgeoning nation. Yet it was all of 300 years before Catholics could be said to possess citizenship in that nation. Economic disabilities pertaining to them — such as restrictions on ownership of land — had been lifted by the end of the eighteenth century. But not until the Emancipation Act of 1829 were Catholics admitted to the franchise and — still with exceptions — to the holding of governmental and other positions of privilege.

Meanwhile, the Church of England performed the historic role of steering the ship of state — the authority of Crown and nation — through the narrow straits bounded by the extremes of religious zeal, the beckoning of Rome on one side and, on the other, the primitivism of the Gospels. Negotiation of this dangerous passage between Romanism and Puritanism confronted Elizabeth I with one of the great hazards of her reign (1558-1603).

Toleration was regarded by none of the contending parties — neither Catholic, Puritan nor Queen — as a worthy expedient. In effect, Pius V (Bull *Regnans in excelsis*, 1570) declared war on Elizabeth, 'the pretended Queen of England, the servant of wickedness', who had 'monstrously usurped the place of Supreme Head of the Church in all England, and the chief authority and jurisdiction thereof'. Invoking 'the fulness of ... apostolic power', Pius declared

> the aforesaid Elizabeth ... to have incurred the sentence of excommunication, and to be cut off from the unity of the Body of Christ. And, moreover, we do declare her to be deprived of her pretended title to the Kingdom ... and also the nobility, subjects and people of the said Kingdom and all others who have in any sort sworn unto her, to be forever absolved from any such oath, and all manner of duty of dominion, allegiance and obedience.
>
> We do command and charge ... that they presume not to obey her, or her orders, mandates and laws; and those which shall do the contrary, we do include them in like sentence of anathema.[5]

Assault on royal authority was not confined to the imprecations of Rome. It was assailed as well at home by a Protestant theology wholly at odds with the Roman. Thomas Cartwright, the most eminent Puritan opponent of the Anglican establishment, regarded Church and State as distinct bodies, yet he left little doubt as to where preponderance lay. Civil magistrates, he declared, might govern only

> according to the rules of God prescribed in his word ... they be
> servants unto the church, and as they rule in the church, so
> they must remember to subject themselves unto the church,
> to submit their sceptres, to throw down their crowns before
> the church, yea, as the prophet speaketh, to lick the dust of the
> feet of the church.[6]

To skirt Charybdis while avoiding Scylla was the task of
John Whitgift, Archbishop of Canterbury, a churchman of
Elizabeth's choosing, he was not so anti-Catholic as to oppose
the hierarchical centring of ecclesiastical authority in the
Crown and could, therefore, be relied upon to stand firm against
the puritanising of religious governance at the congregational
level: 'I perceive no such distinction of the commonwealth and
the Church that they should be counted, as it were, two separate
bodies, governed with diverse laws and diverse magistrates.'
Insistence on uniformity of belief and ceremony precluded any
ministering of the Gospel unless 'according to the laws of the
realm'.[7]

To this end Whitgift promulgated articles of ecclesiastical
governance. The crucial regulation, the sixth — designed to
defend the royal prerogative from encroachment, both domestic and foreign — cemented still further Henry VIII's assertion
of territorial independence some fifty years earlier. Whitgift
would permit none to minister in any capacity unless he first
subscribed

> That her majesty, under God, hath and ought to have the
> sovereignty and rule over all manner of persons born within
> her realms, dominions, and countries, of what estate,
> whether ecclesiastical, or temporal soever they be; and that
> no foreign power, prelate, state or potentate hath or ought to

have any jurisdiction, power, superiority, preeminence, or authority ecclesiastical or spiritual, within her majesty's said realms, dominions, and countries.[8]

Clearly Whitgift leaves no doubt that the power and efficacy of the Crown is uppermost. Yet nationhood in Elizabethan England was not separable from religion. Alliance of Church and State was close, so close as to dictate the smallest detail of religious observance, yet, needless to say, the closeness of the embrace did not signify congeniality. To be sure, the State gained a compliance deemed essential to its unity, while the Church, for its part, could hardly have been indifferent to monopolistic advantage. Beyond such mutuality, however, the intimacy belied the State's vulnerability to religious zeal. Paradoxically, to keep religion at arm's length, the State incorporated the Church into the body politic.

Surprise does not end when one turns to the American treatment of spiritual versus secular allegiance. Adopting a course the very opposite of the English, the founding fathers—for the first time in the history of Christendom—risked a governance detached from the requisites of salvation and devoid of divine sanction. The better to promote national unity, the Federal Constitution separates Church and State (at the national, not yet the state, level). This cutting of the Gordian knot was accomplished with such deftness as to obscure its significance as the culmination of a dichotomy in Western civilisation that began when Jesus evaded the trap meant to elicit denunciation of Caesar's legitimacy.

Initially, the penultimate sentence of the Constitution alone dealt with a problem centuries old, the concluding clause stating simply that 'no religious Test shall ever be required as a Qualification to any Office or public Trust under the United States'. Speaking eloquently to the same point is the Preamble's unrelieved secularity. It proclaims that 'We the People of the United States ... do ordain and establish this Constitution for the United States of America'. The enumerated purposes are eminently mundane: '... in Order to form a more perfect Union, establish Justice, insure domestic Tranquility, provide for the common defence, promote the General Welfare, and secure the blessings of Liberty to ourselves and our Posterity ...' The First Amendment, of course, deals specifically with the question of religion and State. Injunction, however, is negative, not positive. Like speech, press, and assembly, religion is simply off-limits to government. Insulated from secular authority, no faith is to be favoured nor any disputed: 'Congress shall make no law respecting an establishment of religion, or prohibiting the free exercise thereof'.

The taciturnity of this opening clause of the First Amendment belies its import. It says that nationhood must make do with plain fare, that national unity rests not on ideology but on an institutionalised rationality in quest of a security, wholly mundane, defined in a Preamble of but a single sentence. Purpose is uncompromisingly secular; toward religion, the State is neither solicitous nor defensive.[9] This at the national level; but the picture was very different among the several states. At the latter level religious belief affected the prerogatives of citizenship in nearly all of the constitutions newly adopted following the Declaration of Independence. Most common was the religious test for holding office, which appeared in many forms, whether stated in favour of Protestants exclusively, of Trinitarian Christians, of Christians in general, or, still more broadly, of believers in 'a God and the future state of rewards and punishments'. Several constitutions excluded clergy from civil office as inconsistent with a higher calling. The 'Christian Protestant religion' was established in South Carolina in 1778 and so continued until 1790. After prolonged struggle, disestablishment of Congregationalism in Connecticut and

Massachusetts came in 1818 and 1833 respectively. New York's adoption of religious liberty was qualified to the extent that naturalised citizens were obliged to abjure foreign allegiance in all matters ecclesiastical as well as civil. Only in Rhode Island and Virginia was citizenship wholly free of any religious qualification. Each in its own way was cast in a pioneering role.

Persistence of the religious component at the state level was, of course, but an extension of religion's part in fashioning the body politic in colonial times. Inevitably the deep divisions in the mother country spilled over into America. For one thing, a patchwork resulted: Puritanism in Massachusetts, Quakerism in Pennsylvania, Catholicism in Maryland, and Anglicanism in Virginia. Such configuration, however, was not enough to preclude the dilemmas and intransigencies of religious diversity. The founding of Rhode Island (1604) is doubly illustrative. A product of religious dissension in the Massachusetts Bay colony, Rhode Island, for its part, initiated the radical doctrine of religious liberty that was in time to become a noted feature of the American Constitution.

Roger Williams, founder of Rhode Island, was a Puritan for whom man's relation to God required no intermediary but the guidance of conscience. Conscience, however, was not a broad road to salvation; indeed, Williams conceived it as so narrow a path as to render unthinkable a polity consisting of true believers alone. But he did not denigrate the State. Nor did he settle for mere toleration. Instead he placed religion totally outside the purview of civil authority. Such urging of so original a proposition as unqualified separation of Church and State — in the midst of England's seventeenth century passions — testifies to the strength of Williams's convictions, and points to the mixture of thought, theological and humanistic, that underlay his actions.

Theological dispute led to Williams's expulsion from the Massachusetts Bay colony. To be sure, the Bay colonists too were Puritans. But, unlike Williams, they did not scruple against mixing Church and State in pursuit of 'Zion in the wilderness'. Such pursuit — in covenant with God to do His work on earth — entailed theocracy. Massachusetts Bay, regarding itself as a model of purity and purpose, was impatient with conscience and intolerant of dissent. Thus the banishment of Roger Williams.

Williams could well have turned against the State as enemy of conscience. Yet he saw civil authority as legitimate and indispensible, an emphasis that followed from the very freedom that Williams conferred on conscience — such freedom as to render conscience unsuitable as a foundation stone in civil affairs. A secularism of such breadth suggests indifference to theological truth and thus, by some 150 years, to have anticipated the tolerant liberalism of the founding fathers. Yet Williams was intensely religious, a man for whom the spiritual quest was primary, not secondary. He was, to be sure, appalled and revolted at the cruelties of religious persecution; no fanatic, his humanity weighed in favour of civil authority. In any event, however arrived at, his metaphor of the ship at sea is a striking affirmation of secular rule. On behalf of its passengers of whatever faith — including Islamic — Williams would invoke freedom of conscience. None would be forced to ship's prayers nor constrained from his own form of worship. Meanwhile, the captain would be in charge of navigation and his would be the responsibility for the good order of crew and passengers.

Preoccupied as it were with the role of ship's captain, the American Constitution reflects an atmosphere greatly changed from that of the religion-steeped times of Roger Williams. Separation for Williams was in the cause of religion; for the founding fathers it was in the cause of the State: 'its health and prosperity', in the words of James Madison, against the 'malignant influence' of religious factionalism. Because of its secularist bent — not alone its immediacy — Virginia's adoption of religious liberty (1785), not Rhode Island's, was the greater precedent leading to the First Amendment.

To be sure, Virginia's disestablishment of Anglicanism was evocative of Roger Williams' principle of conscience, albeit in its humanistic, not its theological, aspect. Such was clearly so in Madison's opposition to a bill in the Virginia House of Delegates for assessments in support of teachers of the Christian religion. His famed *Memorial and Remonstrance* (1785) holds that religion — 'the duty which we owe to our creator' — must be left to 'conviction and conscience', a right 'unalienable', he says, 'because the opinions of men, depending only on the evidence contemplated in their own minds, cannot follow the dictates of other men'. Yet, having ignored the supernatural, Madison concedes that before 'any man can be considered as a member of civil society, he must be considered a subject of the governor of the universe'. Needless to say, he concludes not for theocracy but its opposite. Paralleling Williams's pragmatism — in contrast to the latter's belief in revealed religion — Madison asserts 'that in matters of religion no man's right is abridged by the institution of civil society; ... religion is wholly exempt from its cognizance'.

Madison painted alliance between Church and State in dark colours. The bill before the legislature implied 'either that the civil magistrate is a competent judge of truth, or that he may employ religion as an engine of civil policy'. 'Arrogant pretension', Madison says of the first, and of the second 'an unhallowed perversion of the means of salvation'. Unhallowed, indeed, is Madison's depiction of the effect on the Church of fifteen centuries of establishment: 'pride and indolence in the clergy; ignorance and servility in the laity'. Nor does the State, for its part, escape the corruption of 'superstition, bigotry, and persecution'. In short, Madison believed that marriage of Church and State could not but debase both parties.

Having successfully opposed the Assessment Bill, Madison

sought positive affirmation of the separation between Church and State. Acccordingly, he moved Thomas Jefferson's bill for Establishing Religious Freedom — first introduced in the Virginia Assembly in 1779 and subsequently laid over from session to session. The Assembly now overcame its hesitancy. The bill was adopted in 1785. Virginia's name was joined to a document of universal importance in the history of political thought.

Prefatory to the enacting clause, Jefferson arrayed arguments in favour of religious liberty. Like Madison, he saw the benefits of liberty primarily in terms of freeing politics from dogmatism and intolerance. He too emphasised history's melancholy experience with establishment: its record of 'temporal punishments' and 'civil incapacitations' which 'tend only to beget habits of hypocrisy and meanness'. On the other hand, as neither Madison nor Jefferson credited the supernatural, both saw — again quoting the latter — 'free argument and debate' as beneficial to religion. Closing on this positive note, Jefferson declared that 'truth is great and will prevail if left to herself', and that 'she is the proper and sufficient antagonist of error'. But the truth here apostrophised is the truth neither of logic nor experiment. It is religion's address to the human predicament and, as such, is the truth of doctrinal belief. There is, therefore, little of ecumenical promise in Jefferson's tribute. Nor does the enacting clause turn on any such expectation, but rather on the avowal that 'the rights here asserted are of the natural rights of mankind'. Accordingly, the Assembly declared:

That no man shall be compelled to frequent or support any religious worship, place or ministry whatsoever, nor shall be enforced, restrained, molested, or burdened in his body or goods, nor shall otherwise suffer on account of his religious opinions or belief; but that all men shall be free to profess, and by argument to maintain, their opinions in matters of religion, and that the same shall in no wise diminish, enlarge, or affect their civil capacities.

Jefferson's epitaph — of his own composition — records three accomplishments: the Declaration of Independence, the founding of the University of Virginia, and the Virginia Statute of Religious Freedom.

Religious liberty in Virginia, impressive as a product of philosophy, was a concession as well to an already existing pluralism. Baptists, Presbyterians and other dissenters had long petitioned against the privileged position of the Episcopal church (not until 1780 were non-Episcopal clergy authorised to perform the ceremony of marriage). A Presbyterian memorial to the Virginia legislature in 1776 serves here as a fitting summary of the American pattern of separation between quests mundane and spiritual:

> We would also humbly represent that the only proper objects of civil government are the happiness and protection of men in their present state of existence, the security of the life, liberty, and the property of the citizens, and to restrain the vicious and to encourage the virtuous, by wholesome laws equally extending to every individual; but that the duty which we owe to our Creator, and the manner of discharging it, can only be directed by reason or conviction, and is nowhere cognizable but at the tribunal of the Universal Judge.

Full emergence of modernity first occurred not in Europe but in America. Even today, the secular purity of the United States is unmatched in those European states with established churches. Notably, however, Italy is no longer among them. As of 1984 a new concordat between the Italian government and the Vatican — a document of historic import — disestablishes the Catholic Church and diminishes its ancient prerogatives in such matters as family law, education, and immunity — variously of property and clergy — from territorial authority. True, where old arrangements still survive, the religious component may well have atrophied. Not so, perhaps, in Northern Ireland and Poland; but in the West generally national consciousness — quite apart from religious belief — now constitutes authority's main support. Indeed, popular sovereignty has achieved currency world-wide. If often failing as sustaining force in actual practice, yet as doctrine the idea does not cease to elicit obeisance. Wishfully, ethnic differences are glossed over in the name of people, while hypocritically, impositions of tyranny are extenuated by the same euphemism.

Meanwhile, the Western state system is still subject to ideological challenge. In the Middle East religion is a force of fundamental political consequence. Communism also is a challenge. Hostile to traditional religion, to be sure, yet, aspiring to a universalism of its own, it too is at odds with the basic principles of the Western state system.

The political map of the Middle East (indeed, of much of the world) is deceptive. Different colours separated by boundary lines give the impression of nation-states on the Western model. But appearance is illusory. Conceivably the states of the Middle East could in time overcome the handicap of recency (none dates before the First, most since the Second, World War) and even of artificiality: boundaries that follow the divisions of the colonial period. However, notoriously unstable, their instability carries a mark of permanence. There is an economic factor: the corrosive effect whether, variously, the corrosion of affluence or of poverty. More importantly, however, is legacy out of the cultural past. The religious mosaic that overlays the area is at odds with the Western state system's assumptions about the nature and allocation of authority.

Of course, religious diversity is not peculiar to the Middle

East, certainly not in comparison to the United States. And yet — more heterogenous not only in religion but racially and ethnically as well — the United States is truly a nation-state. To be sure, the interlaced heterogenity of the United States contrasts sharply with the territorial lodgement of different religious (and ethnic) groups in the Middle East. But patterns of settlement cannot alone explain the different political outcomes. Another contrast, though less tangible, has greater weight.

The American Constitution — as if from exhaustion after centuries of religious strife — seeks peace by differentiating in kind between temporal and spiritual authority and forbidding trespass by one on the other. However, history has denied such expediency to the Middle East. Quite the contrary: clinging to alliance between religion and authority, the Middle East has never known the dualism on which the First Amendment rests. We noted the seamless web of Islam in which religion governs the whole of life. Similarly, orthodox Judaism is a political religion. The Greek Orthodox Church, for its part, was so wedded to Byzantine rule as never — unlike Rome — to have rivalled secular authority. For centuries past the certitudes of orthodoxy, whether Islamic, Judaic, or Christian, not only assuaged cosmic anxiety but penetrated to the very foundation of society's governance.

Encroachment of modernity, centuries-long in the West, is trauma compressed into decades in the Middle East. Identity, based from time immemorial on religion, resists the homogenisation of nation. However sophisticated about their past, peoples of the Middle East cannot escape its tyranny, nor — walking as if on a quaking bog — can governments escape the cross-currents of religion within and across their borders. Two of them, the Lebanese and the Iranian, have foundered. Failing to build a loyalty outside religion, the former collapsed into chaos, while the latter succumbed to the tyranny of fundamentalism. In Lebanon, territorial bounds suffered implosion. In Iran the opposite occurred. There Shi'ite faith — secure enough at home to demand recantation of Baha'is on pain of death — scoffs at territorial confinement and invokes allegiance of fellow believers everywhere. Other governments in the Middle East — all vulnerable to the fate of a Lebanon or an Iran — nervously watch their people and husband military power against threats internal and external, while the wealthy among them warily purvey their largess.

Religion in the Middle East impinges not only on international law. Domestically, too, it has implications for the ordering of society. In neither instance does it yield naturally to the separation of authority into pieces. Pluralism, internationally, exacts the limitations of territorial rule. At home, greater still is impingement on any striving for the amenities of democratic society. Scepticism and tolerance comport ill with the certitudes of doctrine. Yet a sceptical and tolerant outlook — the very hallmark of rationality — is essential to the supreme achievement of a political culture: its acceptance, however paradoxical, of a loyal opposition. Such abiding of an opponent is the great lack of Middle Eastern politics: acceded to perhaps in the abstract, but the modalities of circumscribed authority, whether international or domestic, are beyond the power of mere injunction to effect. Caught in the toils of the past, human rights and fundamental freedoms do little in the Middle East to mediate between top dog and bottom dog.

If Iranian religiosity and American secularity are at extremes of the continuum, Israel is somewhere in between. The tensions of hybridisation are very great. On the one hand, the declaration of 14 May 1948 proclaims the independence of a 'Jewish State', yet at the same time asserts that 'The State of Israel ... will ensure complete equality of social and political rights to all its inhabitants irrespective of religion, race or sex'. Thus, juxtaposed, are foundation stones, religious and secular, of different character. Nor has dilemma diminished over time. In a reflective dispatch (7 July 1984) on completion of a five-year assignment as bureau chief of the *New York Times* in Jerusalem, David K. Shipler focuses on Israel's mounting struggle over what kind of society it is to become: 'religious or secular, nationalistic or humanistic, Western or Middle Eastern, absolutist or pluralistic'.

At the outset, loggerheads in the Jewish community resulted in failure to form a constitution, failure that left unmitigated the danger of polarisation between orthodoxy and modernity.[10] Extremists among the religionists held that 'any Constitution created by man can have no place in Israel' and that 'only the laws of the Torah shall be decisive in all realms of life of the State', whereas the radical secularists would separate Judaism entirely from the workings of State. The cast of the proposed Preamble was rejected by the latter as too strongly religious. Rooted 'in the spiritual tradition which constitutes the timeless heritage of the whole House of Israel', the constitution was said to rest on

> the monotheistic conception of God — invisible, omnipotent, one and indivisible, an embodiment of absolute justice, the Ruler of the universe, the Father of man. The projection of that conception in the moral sphere is an austere code aiming at the sanctification of matter by the creative force of the spirit. Its ultimate goal is the establishment of the Messianic Kingdom, embodying a rule of universal justice freely acknowledged by all the children of men. From its early beginnings, Judaism has aimed not merely at individual perfection, but also at the shaping of a social order. It is concerned not only with the salvation of the soul but also with the political community in which that soul has its roots and being. The great figures of our spiritual tradition were definitely hewn in a political frame. They aspired to the evolution

of 'a kingdom of priests and a holy people', ruled not by kings or priest-kings, as was the practice all over the ancient East, but by the Deity alone — perhaps the boldest effort ever conceived of shaping reality in the image of the absolute. . . . The State of Israel is being rebuilt under modern conditions. It cannot but adopt the institutional forms and civic conceptions by which alone the mass life of a modern political community can be organized. But if these forms and conceptions are to have more than a transient meaning, they must strike roots in the deeper recesses of the soul of the people. It is not by abstract declarations but by the infusion of the Hebrew spiritual tradition into its functional framework that the constitution of Israel can alone be rendered Jewish, can alone be rendered safe.

As between 'Jewish State' and the social and political equality of 'all its inhabitants irrespective of religion, race or sex', the meshing foreseen by the declaration of independence has not occurred. Religious differences among individuals can be subsumed under a common nationality. Not so, however, with differences at the communal level such as are inscribed on the Israeli identity card, which (like the Lebanese), more than nationality, indicates religion as well. Though the electoral process operates across religions, common citizenship in other areas gives way to important discontinuities. Inevitably, separate educational systems differ in language and content. Nor are Muslims subject to conscription in the armed forces. Furthermore, personal status (in matters such as marriage, divorce, adoption, inheritance, etc.) — in continuation of the millet system from Ottoman times — is governed separately by the law and courts of each community, Jewish, Islamic and Christian. In a matter of critical importance to the Jewishness of the state, disjuncture also occurs over prerequisites to citizenship. Criteria applying to Palestinians within the armistice lines of 1949 and to their descendants contrast with the simplicity of the Law of Return whereby immigration alone confers citizenship on the Jew.

Ironically, the very thing, religion, that spells differences of such magnitude as to warrant legal discontinuities along communal lines, does not at the same time ensure unity within Judaism itself. Want of a consensus outside religion plagues relations among Jews as it does between them and the other peoples in Israel. Diversity in the Jewish community ranges from the ultra-orthodox who view the State as enemy of God to the extreme secularists who regard religion as fossilised tradition. Resolution of religion and State having failed at the constitutional level, successive issues have been dealt with legislatively. Compromise has been grudging, turning not on settled principle but on the expediences of coalition politics. Aroused passion over the law's imposition of ritualistic observance of the Sabbath and of dietary rules is hardly less than that engendered by questions more substantive in nature. To the exclusion of the Reform and Conservative branches of Judaism, the Orthodox rabbinate has been institutionalised in the State. Fundamental and sensitive questions arise over Orthodoxy's adherence to religious law (such as the highly charged question of who is a Jew) based on the letter of the Old Testament and over ranking of the sacred texts as the main obligation of education. In short, orthodoxy and modernism are poles around which the alternative futures posed by Shipler tend to form.

Alliance between religion and State, resurgent in today's fundamentalism, has not ceased to invoke the authority of tradition and belief. Nor, needless to say, has secularism ceased to be a potent force. The perennial quest goes on, both spiritual and secular, and thus contest between faith and reason — as if between competing anchors on a storm-tossed ship. Just such dilemma — choice between seeming incompatibilities — is what Karl Marx believed history was in the process of dispelling.

Preached as salvation's one and only anchor, Marxism castigates traditional religion as both superstitious and servile. Instead, casting the human odyssey in secular mould, Marx espoused a philosophy of history. At the same time, notwithstanding, he invested history with a life of its own; a vibrant thing is depicted as sowing and reaping its own future. The process — as if to demystify such dynamism — is characterised as 'materialist'; it centres, Marx said, in the shifting relations among factors comprising the means of production. To their rubbing and clashing he attributed the energising force that propels society on its course.

Not just 'materialist', Marx characterised his depiction as 'scientific'. A characterisation congenial to the intellectual climate of the time, it was a prestigious mantle that served to enhance the credibility of the Marxist creed. Witness to the Industrial Revolution's ruthless reordering of society, Marx recoiled in abhorrence. Dehumanisation — man's separation from nature and aloneness in an impersonal society — stirred so great an indignation as to spurn exhortation as too problematical a remedy. Instead, in quest of certitude, revolutionary zeal rallied history to its side. Marx, in the guise of a detached diagnostician, pictured past revolution as no less natural to man than earthquake to geology and foretold a future uprising of workers as but still another unfolding of the historical process.

Inevitability then takes an unexpected turn. Though still banished by 'scientific materialism', spirit becomes irrepressible and faith triumphant. With a benignity previously unknown, history culminates in Utopia; indeed, justice brings history itself to an end. Authority — the repressive power of State on behalf of privilege — ceases to have purpose and the State withers away. But not immediately. No longer legitimised by subterfuge — neither by God nor people — but vested by history in the proletariat, authority is put to one last use. Needed finally to dispose of the old order, proletarian legitimacy is so clearly manifest as to warrant dictatorship.

As a redemptive belief, Marxism no less than other religions has implications for the ordering of society. That its truth is 'scientific' makes no logical difference in its bearing on authority; like revealed truth, it too is intolerant of pluralism. But, as with all orthodoxies, Marxism cannot but yield to society's complexities. Both domestically and internationally, pluralism resists strangulation.

On the domestic side is the apostacy of those communist parties in the West that have succumbed to the sovereignty of the ballot box. To be sure, so radical a departure from truth's imperatives arouses suspicion of Euro-communism as mere manoeuvre. Yet Marxist prophesy has been so greatly discredited as to tempt communist parties out of power to settle for less than the whole loaf. For parties in power, however, such retreat would be extremely hazardous. To so admit rivals into the political arena would risk the backlash of past monopolisation of power. Yet, communist governments cannot escape the recalcitrancy of a human nature that belies millenniumism. Quandary results; but, however great, it favours holding on to doctrine. Even if no longer sustained by belief, doctrine's continuation is dictated by expediency. Such persistence typifies the dogmatics of conflict — a perversity to which the next chapter will return.

Meanwhile, one encounters the very moralism that Marx sought through science to outmode. Typical of this irony is the tone and content of a keynote address (14 June 1984) by Konstantin Chernenko before the Central Committee of the Communist Party of the Soviet Union. Entitled 'Urgent Questions of the Party's Ideological and Mass-Political Work', it declares the communist goal to be 'the moulding of an ideologically staunch, harmoniously developed and spiritually rich individual who bases his life on the laws of social justice, reason, goodness and beauty'. At the same time 'part and parcel' of forming such a character is a 'most energetic struggle against drunkenness, hooliganism, parasitism, speculation, theft of socialist property, bribe-taking and money-grubbing'. It would be incorrect, Chernenko said, 'to see all of these abnormal phenomena ... as mere "vestiges of the past"'. Indeed, he prefaced a long discourse of sermon-like exhortations by a statement of truly heretical import: 'The revolutionary transformation of society is impossible without changing man himself ... the moulding of the new man is not only an extremely important goal but also the indispensible condition of communist construction'.[8]

On the international side, doctrine is challenged by the pluralism of nationhood — still another awkward manifestation of human nature. Elevating proletarian loyalty above State, doctrine posits two worlds, the one saved, the other yet to know salvation. Thus — similar to Islam's distinction between *dar al-islam* and *dar al-harb* — communism divides the world ideologically into the 'peace zone' and the 'imperialist camp'. A world so conceived is at odds with the Western state system.

Universalism was inherent in the Bolshevist revolution. Struggle with territorial authority has gone on ever since, though once again, complexity mocks pretention. Badly mauled by competing loyalties, communism has made many concessions to the nation-state. True, some communists — some out of sincerity, others expediency — still regard Moscow as cynosure. But there is no longer an organic focus of world revolution. Long since subservient to Soviet policy, the Comintern was abolished in 1943. International meetings — ventured irregularly as factionalism permits — no longer resemble councils of religion but — in accordance with the modalities of the Western state system — consist of representation along national lines among equals.

Tension is very great in Eastern Europe. On the one hand, the norms and procedures of international law apply as if among independent entities. Quite different, on the other hand, are the juridical implications of a 'socialist commonwealth' deemed to be ideologically united. In an address to the Polish Communist Party in November 1968 in the wake of the Soviet invasion of Czechoslovakia, Leonid Brezhnev struggled with the horns of dilemma. Paying obeisance to non-intervention, he said that 'socialist states stand for strict respect for the sovereignty of all countries'. At the cost of a *non sequitur*, he then continued:

> At the same time, affirmation and defense of the sovereignty of states that have taken the path of socialist construction are of special significance to us Communists. The forces of imperialism and reaction are seeking to deprive the people first in one, then another socialist country of the sovereign right they have earned to ensure prosperity for their country and well-being and happiness for the broad working masses by building a society free from all oppression and exploitation. And when encroachments on this right receive a joint rebuff from the socialist camp, the bourgeois propagandists raise the cry of 'defense of sovereignty' and 'non-interference'. It is clear that this is the sheerest deceit and demagoguery on their part. In reality these loud-mouths are concerned not about preserving socialist sovereignty but about destroying it. ...
>
> [I]t is well known, comrades, that there are common natural laws of socialist construction, deviation from which could lead to deviation from socialism as such. And when external and internal forces hostile to socialism try to turn the development of a given socialist country in the direction of restoration of the capitalist system, when a threat arises to the cause of socialism in that country — a threat to the security of the socialist commonwealth as whole — this is no longer

merely a problem for that country's people, but a common problem, the concern of all socialist countries.[12]

Truth being sacrosanct, apostasy cannot be condoned. '[T]riumph of the socialist system in a country can be regarded as final', but, Brezhnev added, 'only if the Communist Party, as the leading force in society, steadfastly pursues a Marxist-Leninist policy in the development of all spheres of a society's life'.

Yet malaise has set in. More profound, traditional religion's assessment of the human condition evokes greater response than promise of perpetual prosperity in a world of perfect harmony. Such surfeit is strangely repellent. Nor has communism fared well in competition with the Western state system. Not the former, but the latter, is the Procrustean bed into which, perforce, today's world is fated to fit.

Tension in society calls forth governance and, coupled with tension in the human psyche, gives rise to religion as well. This intermingling of quests mundane and spiritual never ceases to be at issue. Embattled as enemies and suspicious as allies, religion and State are embroiled even in separation. Yet, demand on others for conformance is not religion's only posture. Conscientious restraint is of quite a different order. We shall note in Chapter 5 (Abraham Lincoln's Second Inaugural above all) that the moral norm, when inwardly directed, does not exacerbate but mitigates conflict. When so disposed, religion does not abet but supresses the power overtone.

Notes

1. Wilcomb E. Washburn, *Red Man's Land, White Man's Land* (New York: Scribner, 1971), Chapter 1 treats in general the legal and theological disputes over the status of the newly discovered Indians.

2. Emperor Chien Lung's mandate to George III may be found in Harley Farnsworth MacNair, *Modern Chinese History: Selected Readings* (Shanghai: Commercial Press, 1923), p. 2ff. For a fuller account of the classical Chinese world view, see John King Fairbank (ed.), *The Chinese World Order* (Cambridge: Harvard University Press, 1968).

3. See MacNair, *Modern Chinese History.*

4. This and subsequent quotations from Vitoria are taken from the section, 'On the Illegitimate Titles for the Reduction of the Aborigines of the New World into the Power of the Spaniards', of his *De Indis et de ivre belli recollections,* ed. and trans. by Ernest Nys (Washington: The Carnegie Institution of Washington, 1917).

5. See Pawel Mills Dawley, *John Whitgift and the English Reformation* (New York: Scribner, 1954).

6. Ibid.

7. Ibid.

8. Ibid.

9. Documents relating to the origins of the First Amendment are conveniently assembled in Anson Phelps Stokes and Leo Peffer, *Church and State in the United States* (New York: Harper and Row, 1950).

10. Discussion of the dispute over the formation of an Israeli constitution is based on Chapter 4 of Norman L. Zucker, *The Coming Crisis in Israel: Private Faith and Public Policy* (Cambridge: MIT Press, 1973). Two more recent treatments of the same subject are Daniel Shimshoni, *Israeli Democracy: The Middle of the Journey* (New York: Free Press, 1982); and Charles S. Liebman and Eliezer Don Yehiya, *Religion and Politics in Israel* (Bloomington: Indiana University Press, 1984).

11. *The Current Digest of the Soviet Press,* vol. XX, no. 46 (4 December 1968).

12. *The Current Digest of the Soviet Press,* vol. XXXV, no. 24 (13 July 1983).

4 THE DOGMATICS OF CONFLICT

Rivalry between spiritual and secular authority and the tensions inherent in the power overtone would occur even though there were no social science to take note of them. Constants that cannot be exorcised, they would persist even without intellectual recognition. Not so the dogmatics of conflict: theories about conflict can themselves cause conflict. Ironically, the very attempt to understand the nature of conflict is itself infested with the power overtone.

Explanations of conflict, whatever the approach, whether sociobiological, psychological, anthropological, theological or that of political theory as such, pose the question of the fixed in human conduct as against the malleable. A fault line runs through each and all of them: the dichotomy of nature versus nurture. The potential for controversy in this apposition is apparent. Debate never ceases as between subjective (inner) and objective (outer) causes. Passionate advocacy, indeed acrimony, attend a matter fraught with practical consequence for choice of policies relating to crime, for example, or poverty: in general, the question of the determinants of behaviour at the point where individual and society converge.

Of course — let it be said at the outset — neither category of cause need exclude the other; society is witness to the interaction, infinitely complex, between nature and nurture. No one denies — anthropology documents — the impact on society of its physical setting: for example, the differing social patterns attributable to climate. But the setting is also cultural: modern adaptation to Alaskan rigour differs from the traditional ways of the Eskimo. Increasingly, man subordinates and exploits his natural environment — to such degree as to induce nature's retaliation against his heedless mastery over it.

But what of man's command over himself? What of human nature? If it is incorrigible, then the only recourse is to bow to its imperatives. Or, if impingement — institutional setting on human nature — runs in the other direction, latitude is afforded for the play of creativity in the moulding of social relations. These different perspectives are fertile ground for the dogmatics of conflict. Biology, psychology, sociology and theology all seek to inform the law-maker, but each betrays a bias of its own. Temperament, too, enters into rivalry between nature and nurture. The idealist, in keeping with his optimism, regards human nature as innately good but subject to the importunities of external circumstance. The realist, less sanguine about human nature and less reform-minded, attributes the imperfections of society to deficiencies inherent in its individual members. These contrasting dispositions lead to widely differing prescriptions: optimists believe in the redemptive power of social reform, whereas sceptics see the only salvation as triumph of the individual over himself.

The dogmatics of conflict would be much mitigated if it were apparent that a progressive rationality is propelling humankind into an ever-improving future. Thus reinforced, a confident social science, increasingly managerial, would look to betterment of objective circumstance. If, on the other hand, human nature is held blameworthy, attention is directed away from behaviour's objective causes to individual endowments and propensities, away from the religious and other institutional frameworks into which the individual is born to his inner promptings, promptings that range all the way from biological instinct to moral sensitivity.

Are patterns of behaviour — instincts from the evolutionary past — embedded in the genes themselves? It is not the purpose here to try to calm the storm raised by sociobiology's answer to this question. Actually the very shrillness of the controversy affords a prime example of the dogmatics of conflict.

Built upon the accumulation of many careful, often ingenious, observations, sociobiology is the study of animal and insect behaviour: the patterns of interaction that give to a species a societal dimension essential to its evolutionary success.[1] Instinctually a colony of termites or a pride of lions or a herd of elephants or a family of apes is socially complex, so much so as to suggest that the sociality of humans too has a genetic component. Conceivably, the emotions, familial solidarity, even the power overtone, are, among others, elements in a human nature inherited out of the distant past. To so assert could well be taken as admonitory — as warning that our ancestral traits threaten survival in an age of science and technology. But it also invites attack. Characterising any part of society as genetically determined has been denounced as a reactionary doctrine lending support to the status quo. Also, inherent in the theory of genetic determinism is a challenge to belief in egalitarianism.

Edward Wilson, founder of the new science of sociobiology, concedes that in humans 'the genes have given away most of their sovereignty'. The passions that he has stirred are therefore all the more noteworthy. His antagonists warn that 'Wilson's gene-dependent culture ... amounts to international racism, implying technologically "backward" cultures have backward genes'. And again: 'It is no accident that the description of this underlying [human] nature bears a remarkable resemblance to the society inhabited by the theorist himself. In Wilson's case it is the modern market-industrial-entrepreneurial society of the United States.'² That these charges should emanate from fellow faculty members of Wilson's at Harvard University is itself testimony to the dogmatics of conflict. Genetic determinism is itself conflict-prone.

Not so neurological illness, whose organic causes can hardly be disputed — such as Alzheimer's disease or schizophrenia. But it is not abnormal behaviour alone that weighs on the side of human nature against nurture. More subtle, psychologically and morally, is behaviour whose normality is itself antisocial.

Actually, the quest for security can be undermined by a psychology that exacerbates the very dangers that the quest seeks to abate, yet is so common to humankind that it must be regarded as more normal than abnormal. Reacting defensively to the outside world, seeking to assuage fear and to enhance self-esteem, it operates at the level of the unconscious and distorts reality. Various of its mechanisms have been identified: *displaced aggression*, or scapegoating, whereby aggression is displaced away from the source of frustration onto some innocent person, group or object; *projection*, whereby an undesirable trait in oneself is attributed to another person or group accused of hostile intent; and *rationalisation*, whereby one reduces anxiety and maintains self-esteem by explaining in acceptable ways actions that are in fact based on unacceptable motives. Then there is the mechanism of the *mirror image* — often present in international conflict — whereby each side, regarding itself as peaceful, sees its reverse in the other and reacts fearfully to what it perceives as aggressive intent.

It would be salutary if these perversities, universally prevalent, were more often dragged out of the unconscious into the light of day. Instead, however, psychological maladjustment attributable to upbringing has caught the greater attention, whether it be the childhood experience of a particular individual, or experience shared with others by virtue of the customary practices of a particular society in the rearing of its young. One strongly suspects a connection between the child and the adult, yet the speculative nature of the psychological link persists. Controversy abounds, whether inquiry centres on the individual or on society as a whole.

For example, discussion swirls around the unlikely figure of Woodrow Wilson — whose scholarly vocation might be expected to militate against any charge of irrationality. To be sure, however much the social scientist, Wilson's judgement could not but reflect the parochialism of the American political culture. Too readily, he regarded self-determination and democratic rule as the evolutionary product of man's past and the promise of his future. Even so, the treatment of Wilson's (typically American) idealism by Sigmund Freud and William Bullitt in their *Thomas Woodrow Wilson: A Psychological Study* is wildly off the mark. Only animus can explain their grotesque allegations, while contradictory and mutually exclusive charges against Wilson as peacemaker at Paris suggest that their collaboration in the making of this strange book was anything but close. The accusation that Wilson assumed the mantle of Jesus Christ would seem to have come from Freud, who — like Clemenceau — harboured old-world condescension toward Wilson's reformism, while undoubtedly it was Bullitt, the American, who was prepared to believe that Wilson's personality (effeminate and acquiescent was the flagrantly erroneous charge) was all that stood in the way of the realisation of his Fourteen Points.

The humiliation of Germany, the yielding to French feelings of fear and revenge, the surrender to Italian territorial greed and to Japanese imperial ambition, all were aspects of the Versailles Treaty that Wilson fought against at a telling cost to his own fragile health. The Treaty's vengeance and its departures from self-determination prompted Wilson to proclaim the promise of rectification contained in the League of Nations, yet he lost all by refusing to compromise with the Senate over the concept of collective security as formulated in Article X of the League Covenant. The question here is whether Wilson's adamancy — over and above intellectual and tactical considerations — was psychologically inspired.

That this and other crises in Wilson's career are to be so regarded is the contention of Alexander and Juliette George in their much cited *Woodrow Wilson and Colonel House: A Personality Study* (1956). The fiasco over the Versailles Treaty is foreseen by the Georges in the difficulties that overtook Wilson's presidency at Princeton, in those that marked the second year of his New Jersey governorship and in the break with his long-time intimate adviser and friend, Colonel House. After their parting in Paris in June 1919, the President and House were never again to meet. All subsequent attempts by House to re-establish communication were rebuffed.

Wilson's personality, the Georges contend, was shaped and deeply affected by relations with his father. The Reverend Joseph Ruggles Wilson, a leader in the southern Presbyterian church, a man of intellect and wit, and of quick, forceful expression, was a model worthy of a son's emulation. In time Wilson was to prove himself equal to the challenge. Meanwhile — so the Georges conjectured — the father's was a daunting example that stirred feelings of inadequacy and self-doubt in the son, the more so because of the standards of perfection to which, allegedly, he was held on pain of ridicule. Thus it was, the Georges believe, that Wilson developed an ambivalence toward his father. Expressions of admiration and love — which the Georges regard as unduly filial — are seen as masking envy and resentment, feelings all the more corrosive because, unwelcomed and unacknowledged, they were suppressed in the subconscious. Thus conditioned in childhood, the adult might be expected to bridle against any subsequent threats to his ego.

To such a pathology the Georges attribute Wilson's stubborn, uncompromising, and in the end catastrophic struggle with Senator Henry Cabot Lodge over ratification of the Versailles Treaty. Frustration, they contend, targeted Lodge for an unwonted discharge of hostility that sprang from Wilson's long suppressed feeling of revolt against his father.

The hypothesis, however, does not rule out alternative conjectures. The confrontation can be seen as an all too common display of the power overtone, as a clash of wills — unmindful of consequences — that readily takes on a life of its own. Certainly Lodge was not an innocent victim of another's provocation. Like his fellow Republican Theodore Roosevelt, he never ceased to nurse an unconcealed dislike — indeed scorn — for Wilson. That Wilson — refusing to compromise despite virtually unanimous counsel to do so — should have responded in kind is an instance of human nature whose credibility does not need to be rooted in the traumas of growing up. But sheer obstinacy, whatever its origin, probably fails to do justice to the complexity of Wilson's motivation. He must have sensed with dismay that any dilution of Article X of the Covenant was but the beginning of a regression into the past and away from the new future that he had held out as the supreme justification for leading the nation into war.

As for Wilson's break with House, the Georges' thesis is hardly relevant. More simply, the estrangement can be explained in terms of House's conduct of negotiations in Paris during the interval in which Wilson was back in the United States. On his return to the Conference, Wilson found that House — of a compromising disposition — had departed from Wilson's explicit instructions, in matters — again — touching Wilson's sensitivity over the fate of his war aims.

There can be no doubt of a highly complex personality marked by a strong will of tenacious purpose. But only conjecture, nothing more, can see the origins of a tragic denouement in such avowals of filial devotion as that contained in the dedication to *Congressional Government* (Wilson's first book, published in 1885): 'To His Father, the patient guide of his youth, the gracious companion of his manhood, his best instructor and most lenient critic, this book is affectionately dedicated by the author.'

Does this hide something? The tone of the dedication and of other such protestations is seen by the Georges as indicative of an ambivalence, the prime evidence for which they trace back to the learning problems that attended Wilson's childhood. It is, of course, known that young Woodrow did not learn the alphabet until he was nine and that he was eleven before he could read with even minimal facility. The Georges' interpretation is psychological. The boy, they assert, was refusing to learn; he was defiant, expressing unconscious resentment against a too demanding parent. Yet a quite different theory is no less persuasive. It sees evidence, not of emotional compensation, but of developmental dyslexia, a neurological problem caused by delay in the establishment of the dominance for language of one cerebral hemisphere over the other.[3]

Such scrutiny of childhood as that of Wilson's now has its own specialised journal: *History of Childhood Quarterly.* American presidents are particularly inviting as subjects, a whole issue being devoted to Jimmy Carter. Allegedly, it was a distant and ambivalent relation with his mother that prompted Carter to seek in political life the affection that he had craved as a child. the opening essay goes farther still. Almost every president, the author asserts, has had 'an emotional distancing mother'. The result is 'a deep hole in the pit of their stomachs', which they are driven to fill with the adulation of the populace. Books, too, have been written. In *Nixon: The Shaping of His Character*, Fawn Brodie contends that Nixon's personality was warped by a coarse, brutal father and a love-withholding mother.[4] A sceptic opens his review of the book with the general observation that: 'Psychohistory is the game in which any player can score at will, because there is no opposing player on the field.'[5]

More sweeping in implication than the individual case are the child-rearing patterns common to a sociery as a whole. Cultural differences across the spectrum of human societies in this — as in every — respect are very great, ranging from wholly customary ways of living together to the intervention of philosophical principles and scientific findings. The differences, moreover, are consequential; some patterns are superior to others, though the question of comparative worth never fails to stir controversy. Interest and vanity combine to admit the power overtone into the comparison: the scientific versus a religious depiction of the world, for example, or a market versus command economy. So too with child-rearing patterns. Their treatment is highly susceptible to ulterior purpose, inviting the charge of ideological predilection even as regards the elemental act of factual description. Such is the allegation of Derek Freeman in *Margaret Mead and Samoa: The Making and Unmaking of an Anthropological Myth* (1983).

Widely read in many languages, Mead's *Coming of Age in Samoa* (1928) bespeaks the potential for influence inherent in social science by virtue of its presumed objectivity. Far beyond academe, the book influenced attitudes and policy and contributed to the groundwork underlying feminism and the sexual revolution. Its main import — the plasticity of society — is enunciated in a foreword by Franz Boaz. Well known as a proponent of cultural determinism, he was Mead's mentor at Columbia University. He said of her work: 'The results of her painstaking investigation confirm the suspicion long held by anthropologists, that much of what we ascribe to human nature is no more than a reaction to the restraints put upon us by our civilization.' Depicting Samoa as almost idyllic compared to the tensions and conflicts of the civilised West, Mead concentrated on youth's passage through the adolescent years. As she put it: 'I have tried to answer the question which sent me to Samoa: Are the disturbances which vex our adolescents due to the nature of adolescence itself or to the civilization? Under different conditions does adolescence present a different picture?' It does, Mead reported. Based on an inquiry into the lives of some fifty girls, she concluded that adolescence in Samoa

> represented no period of crisis or stress, but was instead an orderly development of a set of slowly maturing interests and activities. The girls' minds were perplexed by no conflicts, troubled by no philosophical queries, beset by no remote ambitions. To live as a girl with many lovers as long as possible and then to marry in one's own village, near one's own relatives and to have many children, these were uniform and satisfying ambitions.

In general, Mead described a gentle, peaceful people, free of serious conflict and devoid of jealousy.

Freeman's picture is very different. He found high rates of homicide and assault. The incidence of rape, he asserts, is among the highest in the world. Competitive and prone to jealousy, the Samoans, he reports, live in an authoritarian system conducive to psychological stress, even suicide. In sharp contrast to Mead's finding of sexual pleasure without guilt, Freeman states that 'the cult of female virginity is probably carried to a greater extreme than in any other culture known to anthropology'.

Freeman proceeds to the dogmatics of his case when he writes that it was Mead's 'deeply convinced belief in the doctrine of extreme cultural determinism ... that led her to construct an account of Samoa that appeared to substantiate this very doctrine'. Meanwhile, Freeman denies the charge that he is a biological determinist eager to discredit the culturalists. He asserts that ranking either side above the other 'is as silly as saying that the multiplicant is more important than the multiplier in reaching a product' — an analogy that seems to say that, for want of something better, the author settles for a putative equality.

Clearly, of course, disagreement over nature versus nurture is not attributable to social science's lack of a good measuring stick alone. Deeper still are implications for the perennial struggle between conservative and radical, the scepticism of the former favouring order, while the idealism of the latter favours change. In short, theories about the nature of conflict — whether biological, psychological or anthropological — themselves serve as ammunition in the political arena. Ironically, purported solutions become part of the problem. Nor have we as yet explored the full impact on politics of intellectual controversy over the causes of conflict.

Earlier references to moral sensitivity suggest that amidst all the forces pressing upon him, internal and external, the autonomy of the individual needs to be remembered. As a rational being capable of apprehending the human drama, he can by the same token intervene and become party to his own fate. Such, necessarily, is the presumption of social science. Yet misfortune is not attributable merely to neglect of existing knowledge or to lack of discoveries yet to be made. False steps are not alone the kind that yield to increased doses of rationality — to be blamed, as it were, on an imperfect compass capable of improvement. The mishaps of history are not so readily explained nor easily exorcised.

Security's quest is afflicted with irony; as if in mockery of a vaunted intelligence, man is accomplice to his own misadventures. Political endeavour — central to man's nature and his history — is hazardous always: not only risk of combat but threat to moral integrity. Seeking advantage in pursuit of security, while it does not preclude cooperation, is fraught with the ever-present possibility of encroachment of one individual on another or as between groups. The dilemma is one of conscience at the private level and, at the public, one of law: addressed by Christian theology and the American Constitution, each in its own way.

The doctrine of original sin as interpreted and used in Reinhold Niebuhr's potent and widely influential crossing of theology with political philosophy does not depict man as hopelessly depraved.[6] On the contrary, since conscience confers freedom to choose, abjectness cannot excuse unethical conduct. But human nature — though able by its very humanity to transcend and contemplate itself — is flawed. It cannot finally overcome the bias of self-interest and the pride of self-love. Indeed, to claim such virtue — the supreme delusion — is to tempt fate. The power overtone — in the terminology of the present study — is insidious and inescapable. Conceding limits to brotherly love — even to saintliness — Christianity preaches atonement by the grace of God through the redeeming effect of Christ's incarnation, suffering and death.

Though the American Constitution divorces religion from public authority, it too, as befits a document of fundamental import, rests on assumptions about man's nature. In a word, the Constitution is sceptical. Between the lines one perceives misgivings about man's ability — whatever his protestations — to purge himself of selfish concern.

The founding fathers' reading of history made them apprehensive of 'the mischiefs of faction'. Continuing in the *Federalist Papers*, James Madison puts his finger on how the mischief comes about: 'As long as the connection subsists between ... [man's] reason and his self-love, his opinions and his passions will have a reciprocal influence on each other; and the former will be objects to which the latter will attach themselves.'[7] He goes on to say that 'no less an insuperable obstacle to a uniformity of interest', is the 'diversity in the faculties of men from which the rights of property originate'. Thus, 'the latent causes of faction are ... sown in the nature of man'.

In what amounts to a veritable recitation of the power overtone, Madison proceeds to particularise. Factions, he states, are

> brought into different degrees of activity, according to the different circumstances of civil society. A zeal for different opinions concerning religion, concerning Government and many other points, as well of speculation as of practice; an attachment to different leaders ambitiously contending for pre-eminence and power; or to persons of other passions, have in turn divided mankind into parties, inflamed them with mutual animosity, and rendered them much more disposed to vex and oppress each other, than to co-operate for their common good. So strong is this propensity of mankind to fall into mutual animosities, that where no substantial occasion presents itself, the most frivolous and fanciful distinctions have been sufficient to kindle their unfriendly passions, and excite their most violent conflicts.
>
> But the most common and durable sources of factions, has been the various and unequal distribution of property. Those who hold, and those who are without property, have ever formed distinct interests in society. Those who are creditors, and those who are debtors, fall under a like discrimination. A landed interest, a manufacturing interest, a mercantile interest, a monied interest, with many lesser interests, grow up of necessity in civilized nations, and divide them into different classes, actuated by different sentiments and views.

Thus embedded — in the propensities of human nature and the divisions of society — faction, in Madison's belief, is ineradicable. Futility is sure to attend any attempt to inculcate in all citizens 'the same opinions, the same passions, and the same interests'. Not only futility; any such attempt would be at the cost of liberty. Believing that 'the *causes* of faction cannot be removed', he said that relief 'is only to be sought in the means of controlling its *effects*'. (Emphasis is his.) Having thus grasped the nettle, he did not shrink from the consequences. Refusing to apotheosise the will of the people, while equally loath to take refuge in autocratic rule — viewing the Constitution as comprising 'inventions of prudence' — Madison tackled power head-on as the supreme problem of political science: 'You must first enable the government to controul the governed; and in the next place, oblige it to controul itself.'

'[T]he primary controul on the government' is its 'dependence on the people', yet he would guard against a majority tempted by 'schemes of oppression' should 'the impulse and the opportunity be suffered to coincide'. In a passage that Niebuhr must have noted well, Madison declares that as against 'the injustice and violence of individuals' neither 'moral nor religious motives can be relied on as an adequate controul', and, worse still, that such motives 'lose their efficacy in proportion to the number combined together; that is in proportion as their efficacy becomes needful'. Less the theologian than Niebuhr and more the political scientist, Madison readily sees government taking over where morality falters.

But not just any government. Not pure democracy. Madison warns that so simple and necessarily so small a system responds too readily and uncritically to majority vote. To avoid such a danger and 'at the same time to preserve the spirit and form of popular government', the Constitution envisages representative government: representation of so extensive a territory and numerous a population as to render it 'superior to local prejudices' and conducive to 'the greater security afforded by a greater variety of parties ... against the event of any one party being able to outnumber and oppress the rest'. Representation, moreover, so devised as to preclude the focusing of power at any single point.

Diffusion is first of all geographical: 'The influence of factious leaders may kindle a flame within their particular states, but will be unable to spread a general conflagration through the other states,' whether the cause be 'a religious sect ... a rage for paper money, for an abolition of debts, for an equal division of property, or for any other improper or wicked project'.

Diffusion is also functional: in keeping, thus, with the axiom that the 'accumulation of all powers legislative, executive and judiciary in the same hands, whether of one, a few or many, and whether hereditary, self-appointed, or elective, may justly be pronounced the very definition of tyranny'. General acceptance of this view was such that Madison, far from having to defend separation of powers, felt obliged to justify their overlap. Admitting to 'the encroaching spirit of power', but distrustful of mere 'parchment barriers', Madison argued — in support of checks and balances — that 'security against a gradual concentration of the several powers in the same department ... consists in giving to those who administer each department ... the necessary constitutional means, and personal motives, to resist encroachments of the others. ... Ambition must be made to counteract ambition.' Most to be guarded against was too powerful a legislature. Deploring irresponsible behaviour of state legislatures, Madison admonished the people 'to indulge all their jealousy and exhaust all their precautions' against 'the enterprising ambition' of the legislative branch. Meanwhile, he pointed with approval to the division of Congress into two Houses 'as little connected with each other, as the nature of their common functions, and their common dependence on the society will admit'.

Madison called the architecture of the Philadelphia Convention 'the compound republic of America': the 'power surrendered by the people, is first divided between two distinct governments, and then the portion allotted to each, subdivided among distinct and separate departments. Hence a double security arises to the rights of the people. The different governments will controul each other; at the same time that each will be controuled by itself.'

This is hardly a prescription for radical pursuits. Radical, yes, as political innovators; but the founding fathers were not social reformers. In keeping with a human nature perceived as innately factious, populism was regarded as a threat to be conjured with. Order was primary. Government they regarded as the cement, not the yeast, of society. But there is paradox here. By what path do such predilections lead to the compound republic? The vulnerability of the social order to self-interest does not prepare one for anomaly: for the subjection of the governed to their own consent.

No more than Thomas Hobbes was Madison disposed to trust an unrestrained human nature. Like Hobbes, he too believed in society's need for discipline. Though rejected, the Hobbesian solution was well enough known; indeed, *The Leviathan* could not have failed to make an impression: the weight of precedent favoured the monarchial prescription, while heightened — not crippled — authority would seem to be the logical answer to factionalism. It is not, then, the Hobbesian alternative of unfettered sovereignty that calls for particular comment, but rather the Madisonian innovation favouring its dismemberment.

In diagnostic agreement, Hobbes and Madison are similar in prescription as well in that both centre on the means, not the ends, of governmental action. Yet, though circumscribed, their differences are acute. Whereas Hobbes, for the sake of order, willingly pays the price of absolutism, Madison believes that the remedy need not entail loss of liberty, a cost 'worse than the disease'. Power, even if in governmental guise, is not above suspicion. As a first precaution against its abuse, the fathers based legitimacy in the consent of the governed. (Arguing in the *Federalist Papers* for ratification of the Constitution by conventions instead of legislatures, Hamilton refers to the people's consent as the 'pure original fountain of all legitimate authority'.[8]) This, to be sure, at the risk of populism, but a risk hedged, in its turn, by the compound republic: structured in a stark, spare document concerned solely with the allocation of authority — with permissions and prohibitions on the uses of government. A taciturn exercise in political science became not only the legal cornerstone but the reverential support of a national edifice. Without the prop of religious sanction, the Constitution rests wholly on secular authority; a secularism, moreover, that is unadorned in every respect. Apart from a preamble remarkable for its generality and brevity, the Constitution is stonily silent about the shape of the future. Nor are the *Federalist Papers* any less austere. Madison's scepticism shrank from dangling an ideal future as justification for exacting today's obedience. Nowhere does he conjure up an ultimate goal — a historical destination — to which in 'universal ardor' all else would be subordinate. Here Madison and Hobbes again converge. Neither offers a palliative. Both steadfastly stick to means as the centrepiece of a political system.[8]

Democratic government stands high on the scale of social complexity: such manner of making decisions as to assert authority efficaciously without precluding its future accessibility to today's losers. Ideologically, such a system rejects the prospect of a culminating goal, while psychologically, it gives countenance to an adversary, admitting of his loyalty even in opposition. These attitudes do not come easily; regard for scepticism and tolerance as virtues can only be the mark of a sophisticated political culture.

Whereas democracy is confined to means, absolutism's point of departure is not so narrowly restricted. Confident in its ability to prevail — whether through fear or benevolence — power is wont to flout its detractors. Nor is Hobbes the only possible ally. Karl Marx is another. True, they differ. Hobbes, regarding conflict as subjective in origin, dwells on means, whereas Marx, attributing conflict to objective causes, is concerned with ends. Yet both arrive at an absolutist solution: Hobbes, the conservative, seeks to dispel anarchy; Marx, the revolutionary, to achieve concord.

To be sure, the dictatorship of the proletariat is regarded in Marxian historology as transitory, its rigours necessitated by what precedes and justified by what follows. Attributing inequalities of ownership to a legal system subservient to the bourgeoisie (whereas one recalls that Madison defends property rights as owing to 'diversity in the faculties of men'), Marx predicts a violent sequel. Sovereignty, formerly used to extort, now, in different hands, is used to divest. A triumphant majority — having finally emerged on the stage of history — liquidates the past and establishes an ideal and harmonious future, making an anachronism of coercive authority. Sovereignty ceases to have a function and the state withers away. However, administration remains; all pursuits having become public, bureaucracy is indispensable.

Manipulation of such idealism is easy since both cynical and genuine pursuits alike place a premium on power. The overlap redounds to communism's advantage for, whatever the reality, power covets the garb of good intent. Communist ideology has still another effect in its favour; not only does it mask power but actually absolves it from cause for doubt. By attributing conflict exclusively to society's structure, the communist can depict history as an impersonal process leading ineluctably — so the scenario would have it — to the dawn of a new day. Nor does this dampen his activism. Paradoxically, so to exclude the human element (Marx's 'scientific materialism' scorns the alleged moralism and futility of mere reformism) actually stimulates political endeavour. Blaming society and exculpating the individual energises the latter to revolt. The inner springs of behaviour, by exonerating them of fault, are marshalled thus to help history fulfil its appointed destiny. Perhaps it was just such a grasp of psychological effect that prompted Marx to cast his ideology in deterministic mould.

But at a cost. At the price of an unbridled power overtone. However much Marx the philosopher would be shocked at what Marx the politician has wrought, it is the latter embodiment that today holds some one-third of the world's population in the grip of a rule that mocks its ideological promise, a rule in which all institutions are warped by power, in which all — whether economic, legal, religious, educational, the media — are conscripted into serving ends deemed worthy of whatever means.

A Madisonian critique of power as such is not permitted to break into this vicious circle. Such an acknowledgement of the frailties of human nature would be incompatible with belief in the promised culmination. That which is itself shaped by society cannot be charged with thwarting destiny. Thus logic emboldens power; human nature is depicted optimistically, in a manner consistent with the success of a restructured society.

Such is the compulsion behind 'socialist realism': the test by which communism judges the arts in general and literature in particular. The latter of all the arts is the most explicit in dealing with human conduct and the most sensitive in political implication. In contrast to Western literature's psychological and sociological probings, communist writers are called upon to celebrate the willing dedication of socialist man to the collective good.

Nor is the West alone the target of Soviet literary criticism. The rich corpus of nineteenth-century Russian literature comes under fire as well. Inevitably Fyodor Dostoevsky arouses controversy, as in 1948 when two Soviet biographers

depicted him as a forerunner of revolution. For this portrayal —
the attempt 'to dye ... [Dostoevsky] into a Socialist' — they were
savagely attacked. One critic, placing Dostoevsky 'in the van-
guard of reaction', castigated him for wasting 'the entire force of
his talent on proving the weakness, insignificance and vulgarity
of human nature', thereby lending support to 'the frenzied cam-
paign against man undertaken by Wall Street's literary lackeys'.[9]
Western literature was charged with 'mobilizing all its forces to
bestain and cover with mud all things human', seeking thus 'to
corrupt the souls of men, crush their will to struggle, and justify
the insane violations to which the rulers of the bourgeois world
are subjecting people'. Accordingly — depicted as nursing
within himself 'an evil spider' — man 'must be bridled!'

While this particular instance typifies the arrogance that
Marxism so readily inspires, invasion into the literary world is
an old and familiar manifestation of the power overtone. The
world of science, on the other hand, is less vulnerable. But even
it — the domain of empiricism — is not immune. Not surprisingly, the social sciences are everywhere exposed to
ideological influence. Less so, of course, the natural sciences.
Yet in the Soviet Union psychiatry has not escaped the uses of
politics.[10] Nor has biology.

The Soviet Union was not represented at the sixth World Psychiatric Congress, held in Honolulu in 1977. Withdrawal from
the international body was prompted by mounting protest
abroad over Soviet use of psychiatry to suppress political dissent. Diagnosed as deviant behaviour, dissent was (and
apparently at the time of writing still is) regarded as cause for
committing the nonconformist to a mental institution. Signs
that abhorrence of the practice was about to come to a head at
Honolulu led Soviet psychiatry to the severing beforehand of
relations with its counterparts abroad.

Criticism was not new. Earlier, in 1973, it led to a rebuttal sent
by a group of prominent Soviet psychiatrists to their colleagues

in the West:

> There is a small number of mental cases whose disease, as a result of a mental derangement, paranoia and other psycho-pathological symptoms, can lead them to anti-social actions which fall in the category of those that are prohibited by law, such as disturbance of public order, dissemination of slander, manifestation of aggressive intentions, etc. It is noteworthy that they can do this after preliminary preparations, with 'a cunningly calculated plan of action', as the founder of Russian forensic psychiatry, V.P. Serbsky, who was widely known for his progressive views, wrote. To the people around them such mental cases do not create the impression of being obviously 'insane'. Most often these are persons suffering from schizophrenia or a paranoid pathological development of the personality. Such cases are known well both by Soviet and foreign psychiatrists. The seeming normality of such sick persons when they commit socially dangerous actions is used by anti-Soviet propaganda for slanderous contentions that these persons are not suffering from a mental disorder.

'The seeming normality of such sick persons' is belied by such clinical findings in Soviet psychiatry as 'paranoid reformist delusional ideas', 'uncritical attitude towards his abnormal condition', 'opinions have moralizing character', 'over-estimation of his own personality', and 'poor adaptation to the social environment'.

In 1976 Vladimir Bukovsky was exchanged by the Soviet Union for the Chilean communist leader Luís Corvalán. A dissenter in the cause of human rights, Bukovsky had been declared insane and was committed to a mental hospital. Subsequently in exile, Bukovsky wrote that 'theories and conclusions' in the Soviet Union do not develop out of the raw material of everyday life, but, on the contrary, the raw material ... is created to fit in with the ruling theory. Life does not develop normally and naturally in accordance with its inner laws, but is created artificially in ways calculated not to undermine the basic principles of the ideology.

From where, he asks, does an opponent of communism in a communist society come? 'Within the confines of Communist doctrine there are only two possible explanations; the cause must lie either in subversive activity directed from abroad ... or in mental illness: dissent is just a manifestation of pathological processes in the psyche.' In other words, dissent — inexplicable in terms of the social and political environment — is genetically determined.

As applied biologically by Lysenkoism, environmental and genetical effects are depicted in complete reverse. Polemicist and careerist, the Soviet biologist Lysenko excluded genes as a causal factor in evolution and contended that the acquired characteristics of vegetable and animal organisms are inheritable. Generational variations, he said, 'depend on the ... conditions of life which act upon the living body'. He described his position as 'materialist and dialectical', his opponents' as 'metaphysical and idealist'. Casting controversy thus in Marxian terminology was roundly to discredit the genetic theory.

Argument in terms of ideology attracted Stalin's support. When in 1948 the Central Committee of the Communist Party placed its imprimatur on the environmental theory, holding the genetical to be heterodox, Lysenko's triumph, personal and ideological, was complete. Of course, the weight of science was bound in the end to prevail. But formal disavowal of Lysenkoism did not come until 1964 — tardiness that speaks the potency of the power overtone. More than just a desire to find quick solutions to agricultural problems, the Party perceived a threat to its founding premise: the promise of proletarian dictatorship to mould a new man.

The Central Committee's backing of Lysenko came near the close of a week-long meeting of the Lenin Academy of Agricultural Sciences. Prior to the Committee's intervention, acrimonious exchanges had occurred between Lysenko, President of the Academy and adherents of the genetic theory. Among the latter was P.M. Zhukovsky, who, deploring the rarity of theses on genetics, attributed the lack to the enmities in the profession. Geneticists, he said, 'somewhat fear' their opponents, 'who are very aggressive in their polemics'.

Zhukovsky's recantation (typical of still others) on the day of the Central Committee's published pronouncement is a fascinating example of power prevailing over science. He was not speaking from cowardice, he told the Academy: having decided to make a statement, he had already requested permission to speak the evening before. He then continued:

> There are moments in a man's life, especially in our historic days, which are to him of profound and crucial moral and political significance. This is what I experienced yesterday and today. ...
>
> The speech I made the day before yesterday, at a time when the Central Committee of the Party had drawn a dividing line between the two trends in biological science, was unworthy of a member of the Communist Party and of a Soviet scientist.
>
> I admit that the position I held was wrong. ... A sleepless night helped me to think over my behaviour. ...
>
> I am a man of responsibility, for I am a member of the Stalin Prize Committee of the Council of Ministers and a member of the Committee of Experts on the award of high scientific degrees. I therefore consider that it is my moral duty to be a sincere Michurinist, a sincere Soviet biologist.[11]

It has been said here (and the reproach is deserved) that we do not conduct a fight in the press against foreign reactionaries in the field of biological science. I declare here that I shall conduct that fight, that I attach political importance to it. I consider the time has come when the voice of the Soviet biologists must at last be heard in our scientific press on the subject of the deep ideological abyss that divides us. And only those foreign scientists who realize that the bridge must be thrown from them to us, and not from us to them, can hope to have our attention.

Let the past which divided me from T.D. Lysenko be forgotten. Believe me, that I take this step today as a Party member. As a sincere member of our Party — that is, honestly.[12]

Thus nature versus nurture, an old apposition — a perennial of intellectual controversy — appears on the stage of today's politics, domestic and international. Each of the contrasting premises seeks tactical advantage in combination with power, whether in debate over specific policy prescriptions, or, more generally, in the heat of intellectual dispute. Thus magnified by the power overtone, the nature-versus-nurture dichotomy deepens the chasm of incomprehension between communism and democracy. On the one hand, nurture's optimism abets the use of power in the name of social purpose, while, on the other, nature's scepticism stirs mistrust of power as the instrument of zealotry.

Notes

1. The foundation stone of this discipline is Edward O. Wilson, *Sociobiology* (Cambridge: Harvard University Press, 1975).

2. See 'Sociobiology: Troubled Birth for a New Discipline', *Science*, vol. 191 (19 March 1976); and Edward O. Wilson, *On Human Nature* (Cambridge: Harvard University Press, 1978).

3. See Weinstein, Anderson and Liuk, 'Woodrow Wilson's Political Personality: A Reappraisal', *Political Science Quarterly*, vol. 93 (Winter 1978).

4. Fawn Brodie, *Nixon: The Shaping of His Character* (Norton, 1981).

5. Karl O'Lessker in the *Wall Street Journal*, 8 October 1981.

6. Reinhold Niebuhr, *The Nature and Destiny of Man: A Christian Interpretation* (New York: Scribner, 1964).

7. This and subsequent quotations are taken from the *Federalist Papers*, nos. 47-51 and 10.

8. *Federalist Papers*, no. 22.

9. See 'Readers and Writers in Moscow', *New York Times*, 29 February 1948.

10. Discussion of the political use of psychiatry is based on Sidney Block and Peter Reddaway, *Psychiatric Terror: How Soviet Psychology Is Used to Suppress Dissent* (New York: Basic Books, 1977).

11. Michurin, Lysenko's teacher, was an environmentalist.

12. *Proceedings of the Lenin Academy of Agricultural Sciences of the USSR* (Moscow: Foreign Language Publishing House, 1949).

5 MITIGATION OF CONFLICT

Tension may be unmanageable; antagonism often erupts with shattering effect. This is one side of politics. The other side is society's endeavour to manage conflict, whether by non-coercive or coercive means, from instilling habits of civility to use of force and all the permutations in between: moral norms, legal norms, scientific criteria, diplomacy, ideological conformity and economic pressure.

Of course, social and political (unlike mathematical) problems are never solved. Some conflicts simply diminish over time: desuetude accounts for the contrast between religion in British politics today and its role in the sixteenth and seventeenth centuries. Even so, tension between religion and State, as between all divisions in society (even biological, between generations, for example, or the sexes), is endemic, contained perhaps but never permanently resolved.

Nor is conflict wholly and exclusively counterproductive. Symbiosis between conflict and cooperation was depicted at the beginning of this inquiry as central to man's nature and his history. A stimulant to cooperation (exacting effort as the price of virtue), conflict can also have a positive effect in and of itself. True, the power overtone lurks in readiness to take over. Yet, the danger is not inescapable. Even warfare — however prone to futility and terrible tragedy — can stay within the bounds of useful purpose.

America's violent break with England was not without advantage over peaceful separation. Traitorous defiance of the mother country was a hazardous enterprise. Shared risk strengthened solidarity and the daring of it lived on in collective memory. So too the sacrifice of battle. Those slain did not die in vain. Their's was a poignant remembrance conducive to a unity that — even so — was only narrowly achieved.

The greatest boon, however, was the Declaration of Independence. A crystallisation in terms of human rights and fundamental freedoms, it gave individuality and status to members of a nation destined to become ever more heterogeneous. Reiterated anew in the Gettysburg Address, it survived the fratricide of civil war. At home, the Declaration affords a nationhood tolerant of diversity, while, abroad, that very freedom cements diversity into a common American identity.

The utility of the American Revolution can be measured against Australia's peaceful attainment of independence. Of course, violence alone could not have conferred a new identity in place of the growing irrelevance of the British Crown. Yet absence of trauma — precluding the positive effect that is within the power of conflict to bestow (in contrast to the wholly negative effect of Gallipoli's fearful sacrifice) — leaves Australia groping for a point of departure that, in lieu of revolt, history has not otherwise provided.

Conflict is woven into the very fabric of society; and by the same token society in all its parts seeks to counter the threat. Even so, even though structures outside government (family, church, business, etc.) help to hold society together, governments founder more often than not. Among some fifty at the turn of the century only a few have survived unchanged, while among the plethora of new governments since the Second World War most have collapsed at least once, some twice or thrice.

Yet, however badly battered, society staggers on, meshing its parts and mustering cooperation by processes difficult to discern but sufficient to ward off extinction. True, disintegration may be severe. Among current examples, Lebanon's agony is well known, while history is replete with many others. A depiction some 2,500 years old is as true a picture of anarchy today as it was then. Describing the woes that the Greek world brought down on itself, Thucydides in his *Peloponnesian War* tells us that

> every form of iniquity took root ... by reason of the troubles. The ancient simplicity into which honour so largely entered was laughed down and disappeared; and society became divided into camps in which no man trusted his fellow. To put an end to this, there was neither promise to be depended upon, nor oath that could command respect; but all parties dwelling rather in their calculation upon the hopelessness of a permanent state of things, were more intent upon self-defence than capable of confidence. In this contest the blunter wits were most successful. Apprehensive of their own deficiencies and of the cleverness of their antagonists, they feared to be worsted in debate and to be surprised by the combinations of their more versatile opponents, and so at once boldly had recourse to action: while their adversaries, arrogantly thinking that they should know in time, and that it was unnecessary to secure by action what policy afforded, often fell victims to their want of precaution.

Concluding his famous account of the Corcyran revolution as prototype of the degeneracy that engulfed all of Greece, Thucydides depicts the plight of a lawless society:

> In the confusion into which life was now thrown in the cities,

human nature, always rebelling against the law and now its master, gladly showed itself ungoverned in passion, above respect for justice, and the enemy of all superiority; since revenge would not have been set above religion, and gain above justice, had it not been for the fatal power of envy. Indeed men too often take upon themselves in the prosecution of their revenge to set the example of doing away with those general laws to which all alike can look for salvation in adversity, instead of allowing them to subsist against the day of danger when their aid may be required.

Now as then honour, trust, confidence and lawfulness are qualities whose lack in society is felt and deplored more readily than their presence is appreciated. Their want in today's world is abundantly evident in resort to one-party rule and in the numerous societies that have succumbed to military control. A large majority of the world's population is so governed; which is to say that for the most part conflict is held in check by coercive means: authoritative control over ideas and information, use of economic pressure, and the threat or use of force.

Less tangible is attainment of cooperation without coercion. Or, better perhaps, by indirection only, inasmuch as the backbone of the trust and confidence of which Thucydides speaks are 'those general laws to which all alike can look for salvation in adversity', and the backbone of them, in turn, threat of public sanction. The central importance of law — as a means of coping with the power overtone and of coordinating networks of impersonal relations — needs to be greatly emphasised. But, alone, it is not enough. However impressive architecturally, its efficacy rests on a substratum of political culture affording a degree of trust among strangers (beyond family, clan and tribe) that tempers political competition and invests economic enterprise with confidence. Such disposition cannot be captured in a single formula, nor, historically conditioned, can its emergence in a particular society be easily traced. Amidst the friction of human relations — their animosities and forebodings — trust is a precarious achievement. Short of law's commands, one looks to science for criteria of such demonstrable validity as to prevail by virtue of their own weight. Deeper still — highly important to a democratic culture — is responsiveness to rational and moral influence and practice of an accustomed civility.

Tensions in society have grown with the ceaseless poundings of science and technology. At the same time, however, science has not been without positive effect. In areas such as health and environment, statistical evidence and the findings of the laboratory are often so conclusive that policy (though it may squirm over acid rain, for example, or tobacco) cannot ignore them. Thus — as it were — self-surveillance affords science the means of its own salvation. Even so, scepticism is in order; obedience to objective criteria is itself in need of scrutiny. In less empirically accessible areas such as human aptitudes — where the pigeon-holing of people by psychological tests affects the careers of countless persons in education, business and the armed forces — decision may well suffer from unquestioning submission to the scientific ethos.

Still less can criteria be found ready-made in the social sciences. Not in economics. Afflicted with dilemma, like social science in general, it is torn between choices each of which exacts a price.

Highly corrosive, destitution sets off a scramble for livelihood. Perversely, however, the converse does not follow; prosperity cannot alone give promise of trust and confidence. Material well-being helps, but envy and greed cannot be exorcised from the always continuing struggle between demand for equality on the one hand and for differential rewards on the other. Playing a nediatory role, the discipline of economics moves debate away from the inconclusive ground of justice and fixes attention on productivity instead. Indeed, not unlike the lawyer, the economist has become a fixture in policy-making, private and public, national and international. Yet, lawyer-like — only more so — his counsel is seldom unambiguous. At a loss where to strike a lasting balance among variables hard to detect and even harder to measure, the economist cannot finally escape the culminating dilemma: whether to favour restraints aimed at equality or freedoms deemed to stimulate production.

Clearly, no more than economics do the other social sciences afford the kind of knowledge that tells the engineer how to build a bridge. Of a different order, the social scientist's task, never definitive and never free of predicament, is to weigh choices, whether by way of exposing the waywardness of the politician or of helping the statesman to balance benefits and losses such as to preserve — or better, to increase — society's willingness to live with itself. A bridge, since it cannot serve all interests equally, poses the question of location, a question not of construction but of governance. Conceivably, variables might be so marshalled as to render location less problematical in terms of overall benefit. Yet the social scientist cannot finally rescue the policy-maker from the accusation — if not the reality — of favouritism, or, if not of favouritism, at least of appeasing some sector of society in a loss extraneous to the bridge's location.

Policy's supreme challenge — central above all to political science — is quandary over the future: how best to assure future security without incurring the penalty of an over-extended pursuit of power. Where to place policy on risk's continuum is a crucial question, yet the response of political science is little better than a gamble. In so portentious a matter as an arms race — where reliable prediction of outcomes is badly needed — political science affords not knowledge but at best only wisdom. To be sure, the past yields more than the raw lessons of history; since classical times law and philosophy have had some success in taming the wild beast of politics. Indeed, that such was the political science of the founding fathers attests to a heritage of timeless worth. A discipline of greater managerial assurance would be most welcome, yet political science cannot rid politics of hazard, nor free it of moral ambiguity. Mischance, misjudgement and sheer recklessness, too, all inherent in the struggle of individuals and groups for a secure future, cannot (unlike small-pox) be finally abolished.

Notwithstanding its inconclusiveness, social science is essential to the functioning of a complex society. Data of enormous variety — social and economic — are employed in areas such as welfare, education, budget, taxation and monetary policy, data that, beyond ordinary use, invite sophisticated manipulation as well. Aided by the computer, the social scientist seeks clues to the making of decisions technically correct and of desired social impact — though, needless to say, never with authority equal to that of the natural scientist, nor, for that matter, ever with the satisfaction that his dissections will be used for anything more than partisan advantage. The opinion poll is an impressive triumph, involving knowledge in great depth. Its measurements are used as a weather-vane by the legislator, or, less adventitiously, as direct input into the shaping of social and economic policy. But opinion, notoriously short-sighted, is not a cynosure. A treacherous guide, it discounts the future in favour of today's convenience. However, as an aid to gamesmanship the opinion poll is an unqualified boon. Value-free, it instructs as to tactics and, with increasing sophistication, is used by candidates contending for office and salesmen competing for markets.

Man as author of his own governance — obedient to artefacts of his own making — typifies the stark secularism of the American Constitution. Disregarding historical precedent, it omits divinity from the arsenal of authority. Yet, governance in its nakedness was neither tempted by visions of Utopia nor (unlike the French Revolution) beguiled by presumption of authority free at last to legislate a wholly rational society. Yet, lodged no longer in God, taking refuge neither in a benevolent history nor in the dictates of reason, the Constitution did not fall back on force. Not, to be sure, because human nature was deemed to be well-intentioned. On the contrary, we saw in the last chapter that it feared factionalism and was designed to strangle it. But to no avail. Parties formed and partisanship flourished. Yet prudence was not overwhelmed. Room for self-government remained. Neither rationality, nor morality, nor civility was crowded out.

Double-edged, the Constitution employs reason even as it is wary of unreason. Notwithstanding the threat of populism, trust won over fear and 'We the people' was proclaimed as the seat of sovereignty. This, reason's embrace of popular sovereignty, is not an easy union. To be sure, the American formula is germane to the other democracies; but democracy cannot be transplanted and made to grow at will. Suitable nutrients have not been widely dispersed by a niggardly history.

A product of the eighteenth century's celebration of reason in the wake of religion's excesses, the Constitution, a hand-crafted model of institutionalised rationality, replaced what was little more than an alliance among the newly independent colonies. Yet, even under the Articles of Confederation (1781) — under so unpromising a rule as the unanimity required among the delegations representing the confederated states — a feat of rationality was performed that ranks with the Constitution itself.

The Northwest Ordinance was adopted in 1787 (the year of the Constitutional Convention) by 'the United States in Congress assembled'. Previously, those states among the original thirteen that claimed territory west of the Alleghenies, north of the Ohio and east of the Mississippi (by virtue of their respective grants from the British Crown) had—in an important step leading North America away from a colonialist future — turned all such claims over to the United States. Known to American history as the 'Old Northwest', its governance was prescribed by the Ordinance pending the establishment of new states (Ohio in 1803, Indiana 1816, Illinois 1818, Michigan 1837 and Wisconsin 1848) to be admitted 'to a share in the federal councils on an equal footing with the original States'. Of the same importance to the unitedness of the United States then and subsequently was the provision governing the public lands: 'The legislatures of ... new states, shall never interfere with the primary disposal of the soil by the United States in Congress assembled'. Furthermore, the future Bill of Rights was adumbrated, including religious liberty: 'No person, demeaning himself in a peaceable and orderly manner, shall ever be molested on account of his mode of worship or religious sentiments'. Education was emphasised: 'Religion, morality and knowledge being necessary to good government and the happiness of mankind, schools and the means of education shall forever be encouraged.' To this end (by a previous Ordinance) land dedicated to public schooling was set aside in each township. A notable feature of the Ordinance, especially so in view of the unanimity required among the thirteen states, was the banning of slavery from the Northwest Territory.

Unlike discoveries typical of the laboratory, formulation neither of the Constitution nor the Northwest Ordinance was motivated by the pure pleasure of the exercise. In all such exertions of foresight — however great the satisfaction of putting rationality to work — the stimulus is not academic but practical. Not just for the fun of it, inertia is overcome instead by precaution — precaution against such pitfalls as the past has revealed or the future portends. In short, legislative initiative of whatever kind — whether as constitution, treaty, or ordinary law — is an act of prudence.

To judge morality in the same light may at first seem to be a detraction. Yet, however saintly, moral conduct occurs in a social context — is a tactic of human relations — and to judge it instrumentally from the standpoint of political science is no less appropriate than to treat it as an abstract question of philosophy or theology. Casting ethics into the crucible, politics for that very reason puts character to the supreme test. Indeed, whether meanly or nobly enacted — by a Hitler or a Lincoln — politics, drama unsurpassed, is a morality play staged by history itself. It does not follow, however, that moral precepts are to be regarded as the stuff of discourse between antagonists. Nor, contrariwise, is immorality thereby recommended. The point is that, when confrontational, morality defeats its avowed purpose.

Like the legal norm, the moral norm prescribes conduct. However, if injunction fails, then, unlike the legal norm, there is no appeal to external sanction. Nor does the matter end there. Failure actually exacerbates the conflict. One's opponent is moved not to repentance but to indignation. Predictably, he retaliates. Turning the tables, he accuses his detractor of self-righteousness. Responding to President Reagan's depiction of Moscow as 'the focus of evil in the modern world', an article in *Pravda* by Georgi A. Arbatov (the Soviet Union's leading expert on the United States) charged Mr Reagan with 'frenzied calls ... for crusades that smack of not just the "cold war", but of outright medievalism. And all this is covered up with hypocritical talk about faith and God, about morality, eternal good and eternal evil.'[1]

Making demands in the name of morality inspires a foe's defiance and implicates the accusor's motives. Nor is such encumbrance limited to relations between enemies. Between allies, too, the moral norm is palsied. Admonishing an ally on grounds of humanity poses a perplexity well known to a country as influential and consequential as the United States. Over and over again the question arises whether to settle for immediate advantage or to give precedence to moral standards deemed more conducive to security in the long run. Neither choice, neither expediency nor principle, is assurance against fiasco. The mixing of America and Iran was foredoomed. The clash of values — secular and technological as against fundamentalist and traditional — formed a witches' brew, each culture regarding the other askance, the one with condescension, the other with abhorrence.

If in judging the other fellow the moral norm finds fault more readily than it conciliates, what, then, is its use? How shall prudence prevail? Its conversion into a legal norm is one way. Presumption at the domestic level is that trespass by government on human rights is redressable through an independent judiciary. Such adjudication, needless to say, constitutes a high order of governance. Rare enough domestically, the greater lack is international. True, treaty provisions such as those contained in the Convention on the Status of Refugees (1951) — defining the rights of refugees as regards asylum, employment, education, social security, etc. — are enforceable in domestic courts, whether, as in the United Kingdom by virture of Parliamentary enactment in execution of the treaty, or, as in the United States because such a treaty is self-executing under Article VI of the Constitution ('This Constitution and the Laws of the United States which shall be made in Pursuance thereof; and all Treaties made, or which shall be made, under the Authority of the United States, shall be the supreme Law of the Land; and the Judges in every State shall be bound thereby, any Thing in the Constitution or Law of any State to the Contrary notwithstanding.') On the other hand — through machinery of considerable ingenuity, including a court — the European Convention on the Protection of Human Rights and Fundamental Freedoms (1950) chooses to sanction its obligations at the international level. However, the cluster of European democracies is unique. Government in no other region are prepared to accede to so definitive a scrutiny of their observance of human rights.

Among the purposes of the United Nations, Article I of the Charter includes the 'promoting and encouraging [of] respect for human rights and fundamental freedoms for all without distinction as to race, sex, language, or religion'. Having initially treated the subject in the form of the Universal Declaration of Human Rights (1948), the General Assembly (through the United Nations Commission on Human Rights) then turned to converting declaratory treatment into legal obligation. Eventually, in 1966, it recommended two Covenants for adoption by governments.

Two documents instead of one reflect the central difficulty encountered in nearly two decades of negotiation that followed the Universal Declaration: whether government should be treated as friend or foe. The Covenant on Civil and Political Rights, for its part, contains the proscriptions on government that have evolved out of the long experience of the West in the building of democratic institutions. The Covenant on Economic, Social and Cultural Rights is of a different order. Reflecting not distrust of government but its uses, it speaks of such things as the 'right to work', 'the right of everyone to social security', and the right to 'the highest attainable standard of physical and mental health' These are not individual freedoms capable of legal definition and court enforcement. They are depictions of the general welfare, goals that invite debate over alternative policies, none of which can guarantee the desired outcome. Thus 'the fundamental right of everyone to be free from hunger', unlike a traditional right, elicits not a prohibition but an exhortation; governments are called on 'to improve methods of production, conservation and distribution of food by making full use of technical and scientific knowledge', etc.

Ratified thus far by some 45 governments, the Covenants

entered into force in 1976. Signed on behalf of the United States in 1977 and transmitted to the Senate in 1978, they comprised part of President Carter's emphasis on human rights in the conduct of American foreign policy. But the Senate has yet to give its advice and consent. Incorporation of human rights into international law still awaits American concurrence.

By implication, the Covenant on Economic, Social and Cultural Rights — side-effect to a long and arduous negotiation — attributes to government a prescience and a managerial capacity that betrays ideological supposition. Actually, legal guarantee of a better future seems unlikely to make the stewardship of some 160 sovereign managers any less problematical nor the adoption of so gratuitous a document any more persuasive. It could, of course, have gone unsigned. Instead, the State Department's letter of transmission counselled the Senate to declare the Covenant's substantive provisions to be nothing more than 'goals to be achieved progressively rather than through immediate implementation' and — in a notable example of overkill — to declare that the Covenant was not to be regarded as self-executing. With better reason, the latter precaution was repeated in connection with the Covenant on Civil and Political Rights, whose provisions — eligible for direct application in American courts by virtue of Article VI of the Constitution — would otherwise raise questions of compatability with the Bill of Rights and the long history of their judicial refinement.

Thus, it is not without irony that incorporation of human rights into international law should have been sought largely at America's insistence. In keeping with its domestic success in converting moral into legal norms, the United States pushed human rights beyond the Universal Declaration into the domain of international legal obligation. Yet, the resulting documents turned out to be unsuitable for its unqualified acceptance. Inasmuch as the Soviet Union has subscribed to the Covenants, the irony is greater still.

Compromise teaming ideological differences tandem-style — individual rights with collective purpose — is not the only evidence of struggle in the UN Commission on Human Rights. The Third World made itself felt in the form of identical assertions, comprising Article I of both Covenants, to the effect that 'All peoples have the right of self-determination. By virtue of the right they freely determine their political status and freely pursue their economic, social and cultural development.'

This attempt — twice over — to provide statehood with a common and basic *raison d'être* elicits a worthy proposition. Yet its idealism is suspect. More political than juridical, it reflects a time when empires were under siege and self-determination was everywhere the battle-cry of decolonialisation. The climate has since changed. Vested interest in today's map has shifted focus away from self-determination to territorial integrity instead. Thus members of the Organisation of African Unity — independence achieved — pledge their 'respect for the sovereignty and territorial integrity of each member-state and for its unalienable right to independent existence'.

This 'unalienable right to independent existence' is a formidable claim on the world. And the claimants are numerous. Reason calls for at least a minimal prescription governing so exalted a status — and there are, of course, authentic instances of self-determination. For the greater part, however, state does not embody nation — a lack that the UN cannot remedy by fiat. Moreover, international law is undemanding even as regards the bare essentials of viability. Recognition of new states, whether by government or, collectively, by international organisation, is virtually devoid of guidelines. Historical caprice determines the political map, which jurisprudence then authenticates. Not, to be sure, with iron-clad guarantee. Frailty of political boundaries in Indo-China, Afghanistan and Central America attests to that. Yet, perversely, 'respect for ...

sovereignty and territorial integrity' is such that it shields misconduct of monstrous proportions. Qadhafi endangers neither Libya's membership in the international community nor his own prerogatives as head of state.

Apart from legal formulation of moral injunction, behaviour is susceptible to inner promptings, moulded, as it were, at its own instance. Clearly the quality of such promptings makes a difference, for better or worse, in interpersonal relations. With profound effect, they are also consequential in the broader political domain. A political culture consists not of words alone. Among its many strands is the conduct of its historical figures.

For example, Hitler: his unconscionable use of power in all of its most abhorrent forms in the name of racial superiority and national supremacy. Memory of it is a blight. Like a black cloud, it hangs forever over the writing and teaching of German history. Indeed, over humankind itself.

Or take a different case, the mixing of Napoleon's overweening egotism with national aggrandisement. Unexpiated, conquest was celebrated as nationhood's very essence. France's extravagant entombment of Napoleon (in the saintly company of his fellow generals) — a veritable deification — stands as history's façade to the cult of nationalism.

But human discernment is not to be underestimated. Acclaim greater still — and durable at that — is reserved for conduct the very opposite of Napoleon's. George Washington was a proud man sensible of the veneration accorded him, yet he fended off popular homage and shunned the very appearance of ambition. Victorious at the head of a devoted army and concerned over the fate of the nation whose independence he had won, Washington chose, none the less, to forsake public life. On 19 December 1783, appearing at Annapolis before 'the United States in Congress assembled', he returned his commission into civilian hands:

Mr. President,

The great events on which my resignation depended, having at length taken place, I have now the honour of offering my sincere congratulations to congress, and of presenting myself before them, to surrender into their hands the trust committed to me, and to claim the indulgence of retiring from the service of my country.

Happy in the confirmation of our independence and sovereignty, and pleased with the opportunity afforded the United States of becoming a respectable nation, I resign with satisfaction the appointment I accepted with diffidence; a diffidence in my abilities to accomplish so arduous a task, which however was superseded by a confidence in the recitude of our cause, the support of the supreme power of the union, and the patronage of heaven. ...

Having now finished the work assigned me, I retire from the great theatre of action, and, bidding an affectionate farewell to this august body, under whose orders I have so long acted, I here offer my commission and take my leave of all the employments of public life.

On this occasion of great solemnity and emotion, carefully crafted with history as witness, 'the United States in Congress assembled', addressing Washington in reply, acknowledged the

resignation of the authorities under which you have led their troops with success through a perilous and a doubtful war. Called upon by your country to defend its invaded rights, you accepted the sacred charge, before it had formed alliances, and whilst it was without funds or a government to support you. You have conducted the great military contest with wisdom and fortitude, invariably regarding the rights of the civil power, through all disasters and changes. You have by the love and confidence of your fellow citizens, enabled them to display their martial genius and transmit their fame to posterity. ...

Having defended the standard of liberty in this new world, having taught a lesson useful to those who inflict and to those who feel oppression, you retire from the great theatre of action with the blessings of your fellow citizens. But the glory of your virtues will not terminate with your military command; it will continue to animate remotest ages. ...

It was well understood and fully appreciated that Washington was not indifferent to the nation's future. As seen by his fellow countrymen, resignation was the act of a Cincinnatus, the legendary hero called from his plough to rescue Rome, who returned to his fields when danger had passed. Not an abnegation, Washington's was a dramatic act of republican faith. It preserved and augmented a prestige of enormous consequence for the nation's future, a prestige crucial to the calling of the Constitutional Convention, to the success of its proceedings and to the launching of the ensuing experiment in self-government. As remarked by Gary Wills, Washington 'perfected the art of getting power by giving it away'.

The United States did not enter on its career without defect. An issue uniquely moral grew into a war of 650,000 dead. Yet the philosophy and architecture of the founding fathers survived the ordeal. At the junction between constitution-making and the West's long tradition of political thought, the Union remained intact, indeed, emerged invigorated. For this, posterity is indebted to Abraham Lincoln. Much is owed to the eloquence — the cadence and import — of the Gettysburg Address. The Second Inaugral, too, resounds in national memory — and, like Gettysburg, beyond.[2] The last paragraph has been repeated many times over, while the whole — of some 700 words (spoken six weeks before his death and less than five weeks before war's end) — is a state paper wholly unique.

Lincoln probed the interface between politics and ethics: not as detached philosopher but as President, indeed as Commander-in-Chief.

The war, as befits tragedy, is depicted without blame or triumph. Both parties 'deprecated' its coming, 'but one of them would *make* war rather than let the nation survive; and the other would *accept* war rather than let it perish. And the war came.' Such, in execution of Lincoln's oath of office, was war's immediate cause. But deeper than legal, the cause was moral. 'One eighth of the whole population were colored slaves, not distributed generally over the Union, but localized in the Southern part of it. These slaves constituted a peculiar and powerful interest. All knew that this interest was, somehow, the cause of the war.' Lincoln does not then, as in the Gettysburg Address, universalise the meaning of the war. He sticks to expiation:

> It may seem strange that any men should dare to ask a just God's assistance in wringing their bread from the sweat of other men's faces; but let us judge not that we be not judged. The prayers of both could not be answered; that of neither has been answered fully.

Politics, for its part, is hardly to be regarded as more promising than prayer. But, if the address does not lose character by painting a bright future, neither does it end in disillusion:

> With malice toward none; with charity for all; with firmness in the right, as God gives us to see the right, let us strive on to finish the work we are in; to bind up the nation's wounds; to care for him who shall have borne the battle, and for his widow, and his orphan — to do all which may achieve and cherish a just, and a lasting peace, among ourselves, and with all nations.

'[A]s God gives us to see the right' is not truth's vindication of divine wrath. '[F]irmness', yes, but not without a kindling of doubt such as to combat man's disposition to malice. Against this all-consuming evil, Lincoln admonishes against judging one's enemys and invokes charity instead.

This seeming neglect of righteousness bespeaks not cynicism but a common humanity: none without fault, all worthy of compassion. Such, indeed, is the morality lying behind the conventionalities of polite behaviour. Calculated to buffer the rubbing of egos, civility may seem to favour insincerity over candour. Yet its usefulness as a lubricant not only excuses it on grounds of expedience, but allows for the respect and toleration owing to a fellow creature.

The handling of rebuff is a problem common to all languages; but, a matter of great delicacy, equivalencies are hard to establish. A Japanese writer, remarking that a 'clear-cut expression of one's opinion or sentiment may displease or hurt another', points out that to avoid this 'the Japanese have invented various elaborate expressions, complicated honorifics and deliberately blurred or simplified expressions'.[3] A foreigner testifies to the difficulties that such circumlocution presents:

> For the English speaking person, 'maybe' has a pleasant and useful duality. It exhibits a positive surface, admitting some hope and yet carries unmistakably negative undertones. 'Maybe we'll go', tends to mean that we do not intend to, but don't wish at the moment to completely negate the questioner's hopes. ... The English 'maybe' would seem to be perfectly suited to Japanese requirements, but apparently even it is indelicately clear.

Too negative in weight, translation of the full force of 'maybe' would offend Japanese sensibilities.

Magnanimity and compassion are not uncommon among persons, to the point even of self-sacrifice. Typically, however, forebearance in group relations is regarded as display of weakness. In such circumstances — where the individual speaks not for himself but for others — it follows that the code of conduct will be correspondingly more rigid.

At the international level, today's code differs from virtually all of historical precedent. Past authority, deemed to be divine and universal, was hierarchically structured and called for subordination of inferior to superior. The transition in Europe from this accustomed pattern to one of equality among territorial sovereigns was a slow and wrenching process that eventuated in international law replacing the hierarchical with diplomatic protocol. Etiquette, yes; but, more than superficial, diplomacy's formalities serve to forestall bruised dignity.

The considerable migration of diplomatic privileges and immunities from the persons of European monarchs to today's throng of sovereignties of all manner and clime has not been without wear and tear. Always a slender reed — pitted against the ambitions and anxieties of power — they are today a poor match for the ease of electronic eavesdropping. Nor are their tribulations technological only.

Sovereignty has never been highly discriminating in its choice of hosts, yet it has seldom shielded chicanery to equal the enterprise of the North Korean embassy in Denmark. Needing money, it imported tobacco and drugs under diplomatic seal for sale on the black market. Meanwhile, the least of Libya's tampering with the customs and usages of the Western state system is the renaming of its embassies. Now called 'People's Bureaux', the new name testifies to popular sovereignty's penetration into today's beliefs about legitimacy. Actually, of course, as outposts of a regime centred in the person of Qadhafi, they are engaged in murderous pursuit of the Colonel's enemies and, in turn, are stalked by them. Befuddled, host countries continue to accord to precinct and personnel the singular advantages of diplomatic status.

However, greater than crime's impact on diplomacy is the Bolshevist revolution's positing of two worlds. impugning the justice of non-communist authority implies an ineradicable enmity that invites fear and condones suspicion. Espionage, necessary and natural to Comintern intent, rapidly engulfed all Soviet establishments abroad. Nor has the inviolability of international organisation withstood invasion. The inability of the UN Secretariat to digest its communist component helps to explain the contrast between it and the bureaucratic efficiency and loyalty that the more homogeneous League of Nations achieved under the leadership of Sir Eric Drummond.

Nor has infection stopped there. Obeying the political analogue of the law that bad money drives out good, it has spread further still. Fear's weakening of democracy's inclination to live and let live excuses actions that would otherwise be regarded as insupportable. The United States is particularly at risk. The futility of 58,000 lives lost in the morass of Indo-China's politics testifies to the degree of sacrifice that its super-power status evokes. Nor is battle's the only exaction. No less lethal is compulsion of a different order. Insulated from the power politics of the nineteenth century, America's accustomed innocence magnifies today's departures from the ethics of democratic conduct. Such departure stands out in the instance of the CIAs mining of Nicaraguan harbours, a reckless act, but above all one that Nicaragua contrived to take to the World Court. Stunned, the United States responded to the Court's summons on the preliminary question of jurisdiction, complying thus with the requirement of the founding Statute ('In the event of a dispute as to whether the Court has any jurisdiction, the matter shall be settled by the decision of the Court').

However, its arguments did not prevail; the Court in a procedural finding of 26 November 1984 took jurisdiction. Whereupon, in a statement of 18 January 1985, the State Department declared the Court's action to be 'contrary to law and fact', and announced that with 'great reluctance, the United States has decided not to participate in further proceedings in this case'. Thus, though the mining quickly ceased under protest from third parties, fiasco spread. Twice over, American prestige was damaged: from the foolhardiness of the act itself and from cavalier treatment of the Court. Nor, unfortunately, has any credit accrued to the Court by virtue of the positive nature of its action. Any such profit is negated by the notoriety of the American rebuff. Indeed, not just faulting the Court for 'overreaching', the statement sounds an ominous note. Meant as vindication by indirection, yet it expresses the genuine worry of one of the Court's principal founders:

We have seen in the United Nations, in the last decade or more, how international organizations have become more and more politicized against the interests of the Western democracies. It would be a tragedy if these trends were to infect the International Court of Justice. We hope this will not happen, because a politicized Court would mean the end of the Court as a serious, respected institution. Such a result would do grievous harm to the goal of the rule of law.

Means subordinated to ends, common to technology, criminality and ideology alike — all signs of deterioration in peacetime constraint — is greater still in terrorism, deterioration's most recent and most shocking manifestation. Equated by its perpetrators with society's shortcomings, its discharge of rage — in part, of course, psychopathic — relates to circumstances both specific and general. The poisonous vapours of Middle Eastern politics — its clash of religions and of religion with modernity — have spread outward, as have repercussions of other trouble spots, while, more broadly, terrorism, abetted by ideology, is favoured by the fragility of technological civilisation and sheltered by the connivance of willing sovereignties. By virtue of its pervasive influence, the United States was target of some thousand incidents of terror between 1969 and 1981, while, in the fifteen years as of 1983, 27 State Department people, including five ambassadors, were killed.

Yet, however battered its accustomed status under international law, the diplomatic pattern is still basic to relations between nations. Modified, to be sure; by juridical invention among the democracies of Western Europe and, in Eastern Europe, by Soviet hegemony in the guise of a socialist commonwealth. Much less so, however, by the United Nations, whose observance of the Charter principle of 'sovereign equality of all its Members' has, willy-nilly, grown stronger through the years — and the Organisation correspondingly weaker. Indiscriminate proliferation in membership — the unforseen fallout of decolonialisation — has resulted in the adoption of resolutions whose majority support is of little effect without inclusion of those members on whose exertion, financial or otherwise, implementation depends. Thus, as the century draws to a close, neither displacement nor ridicule pose a serious threat to the basic pattern of equality among sovereigns. Nor is the continuing separateness of authorities owing merely to cultural lag. It comports with the great diversity in the world: the vast differences, for example, between the Soviet Union and Great Britain, the United States and Mexico, or Japan and China. Paradoxically, the function of international law is not only to pull the world together but to keep unlike things apart.

In short, not integration, but dealing at arm's length is appropriate to diversity. To be sure, the art of diplomacy, butt of many cynical aphorisms, is not properly appreciated. Prone to compromise — not a win-all, lose-all game — it blunts appeals to justice and lacks the excitement of a gamble. Scorned as unprincipled, yet it recognises that politics (for example, the repeatedly fought over and still unresolved question of succession to Britain's Palestine mandate) cannot be reduced to the morality and legality of normative solutions. True, difference in bargaining power invites exploitation of the weak. At the same time, estimate of relative strength is a difficult and unreliable calculation that often goes wrong. Nor is a clearly one-sided advantage guarantee against folly. The vindictiveness of Versailles taught a lesson too painful to ignore. Following the Second World War, exemplary diplomacy surmounted the perils of unconditional surrender and rehabilitated a prostrate world.

A specific example helps to illustrate diplomacy's triumph the second time around. As drawn by the Italian peace treaty of 1946 and subsequently adjusted by direct negotiation, the boundary between Italy and Yugoslavia shows promise of permanence. The return of Trieste to Italy in 1954 (the peace treaty had made it a free city under UN governance) helped to dispel umbrage over a boundary otherwise imposed by defeat. Of course, even at best, a mutually satisfactory settlement was impossible. Resolvable neither by moral nor legal norms, neither was the dispute amenable to the politically suspect statistics of successive censuses. Yet an open sore bequeathed by the First World War has been healed with reasonable finality by the arbitrament of war and the solace of diplomacy.

More than mere formality and not just between governments, diplomacy operates at all levels of human relations. Whether between individuals or within and between groups of every kind and variety, wherever parties negotiate as equals, neither claiming superiority over the other, where, in other words, autonomy is mutually recognised, all the great multitude of such reciprocal relations are diplomatic in kind.

Nor — second only to the legal norm in consequence — is diplomacy's a minor role. Flight into rigidity — such as, lasting for more than two centuries, Japan's self-imposed isolation — is today impossible. The comforts of conventional society are nowhere to be had. All arenas, from family to commonwealth, are in flux. Outgrown, tradition can no longer ward off negotiation, while legislation vacillates, uncertain as to where the law's generalities should defer to a situation's peculiarities: where, in short, regulation should give way to parley. Locating such a line emerges everywhere as a central issue of public policy. To be sure, ideology, from libertarianism to communism, has not failed to enter the lists; dogma runs the whole gamut of matters social, economic and political. Inescapably, however, dogma clashes with pragmatism: authority's finality with negotiation's uncertainty. Increasingly, as evidence grows of society's erratic response to government's bureaucratic helm, balancing decisions public and private becomes an acknowledged need.

But, incapable of arousing enthusiasm, pragmatism is an uphill battle. Rivalry between command and market economies persists. Flouting the tests of trial and error, it is the favoured rallying point of today's politics. How so prosaic a matter has gained so great a prominence, domestically and internationally, is a story that begins with reason's belief in the capacity of a desanctified, secularised authority to legislate the future. In contrast to Adam Smith's unruly sea of negotiation, a planned and administered economy promises efficiency and contains vision of a just society based on equality. Stripped of its philosophy of history, this — confidence in the efficacy and justice of a centralised intelligence — is the kernel of Soviet Marxism. It distrusts manoeuvre and compromise as disruptive and regards negotiation as a temptation harmful to individual and the greater good alike. Highly articulated, it differs from the loose jointedness of Western democracy, above all in contrast to the American. The latter, emphasising not the community but the individual, preaches enterprise as a virtue, actually pushing the individual into negotiating his way through life. The contrast is brought our by Shevchenko in his *Breaking with Moscow*:

> It puzzles them [Soviet leaders] how a complex and little-regulated society can maintain such a high level of production, efficiency and technological innovation. Many are inclined toward the fantastic notion that there must be a secret control center somewhere in the U.S. They continue to chew on Lenin's dogma that bourgeois governments are just the 'servants' of monoply capital.

Puzzlement extends more broadly still:

> While intrigued by American freedoms, political plurality and cultural diversity, the Soviet leadership is unable to comprehen fully the mechanism of the U.S. political system. there is little grasp of the relationship of American Congressment to their constituencies, the real role of public opinion and than worst bugaboo, freedon of information, which they see as a threat to security.

But if there is peril in rigidity so too in liquidity. If human relations were negotiable without cease, lack of predictability would threaten society's dissolution. Such was the turmoil of the Great Proletarian Cultural Revolution. Paradoxically — his fondness for precept more Confucian than Marxian — Mao Ze-Dong's idealistic impulse was to reinvigorate recolution's assault on traditional Chinese culture. Innumberable episodes depict a nihilism to which youth in particular was addicted and that spread to the universities with lethal results. Ten students were killed at Tsinghua University when the Red Guard won control and began 'cleansing' thought and re-educating professors and students. This went forward without restraint for some months ... but ... the Red Guards split into two factions, each of which regarded itself as the pure defender of Maoist theory and the other as made up of traitorous renegades ...

The groups armed themselves not only with rifles but also with grenades, which they made in the laboratories and even with ... rockets and mortars, which they made in the machine shops. One faction built a primitive tank. ...

[S]tudents, unable to overwhelm each other by direct assault, went underground and dug tunnels, hoping to get access to each other's buildings or to blow them up. None of the efforts succeeded, but the science building was gutted by fire bombs and dormitories were badly battered.[4]

In still another episode described as 'irrational gang warfare', students at Peking University, unable to get guns, resorted to 'spears, catapults and iron bars and protected themselves ... with home-made body armour and helmets'.

A big battle took place ... when the Chingkangshan Regiment attempted to capture two buildings occupied by the New Peking University commune.

When Miss Nieh Yuan-tzu, noted Maoist ... in the philosophy department of Peking University, intervened to stop the fighting ... she was stabbed in the back by someone from the Chingkangshan faction.

Miss Nieh apparently was not badly hurt because she attended a meeting later in the evening at which the Chingkangshan students rejected a demand that they produce the assailant.

[F]ighting ... [continued] sporadically ... [T]wo students were killed and their bodies put on public display ...[5]

The immanence of violence is a threat, ever present, with which society wrestles unceasingly. Its manner of doing so ranges across the spectrum from ruthless suppression of dissent to the disciplining of authority itself. In between, between authority without stint and authority under constitutional constraint, is the great body of substantive and procedural law.

Relevant to conflict's mitigation is the actual economic and social content of the law. No less important, however, is its procedural side. Common to the evolutionary development of both Roman and common law, it consists in two features of the utmost consequence for society's management of conflict, involving first a conceptual differentiation between matters public and private and second, dependent thereon, sharply different procedures for invoking the law.

Health, safety, and the general welfare became part of the first category and the state learned to take the initiative in protecting the public in these matters of common concern. Through its police power, the state apprehends, prosecutes and punishes. By virtue of taking such responsibility, authority protects society against a great danger: against the compulsion of individuals and groups to measure their relations in terms of power alone.

Less direct than its intervention in criminal matters, but no less consequential for thwarting the power overtone, is the role of the state in civil disputes. As between private parties, the law has much to say, but it remains for the plaintiff to invoke it. Typically, the loser, whether plaintiff or defendant, disagrees volubly with the judgement of the Court. Frequently he appeals to a higher court. But in the end he must submit. His one consolation is to attribute submission to the authority of the Court — not to the will of his adversary but to the intervention of a third party — a consolation as important to society's good order as to the salving of his pride.

At the international level, such adjudication as occurs is

but, of course, not by virtue of criminal but only civil jurisdiction. Two courts stand out, the World Court and the Court of Justice of the European Community. Highly developed, the jurisdiction of the latter is not only compulsory; parties with standing before it, whether as plaintiff or defendant, include, along with states, organs of the European Community, corporate entities and natural persons. The World Court possesses no compulsory jurisdiction by virtue of its founding treaty; what little it has is based solely on supplementary acts of its members. And only states have standing before it in contentious cases — though, to be sure, organs of the United Nations may solicit advisory opinions.

If sovereignty's acquiescence to adjudication has been meagre, it is hardly surprising that police power at the international level should have fared worse still. Collective security, twice over, has failed to establish a centre of authority and power capable of rescuing international politics from the toils of the power overtone.

The limited warfare of the eighteenth century bore a meaningful relationship to the attainment of political goals. As war has since become increasingly total and as its meaningfulness as an instrument of policy has steadily declined, it is ironical — testimony to the perversity of politics — that the sacrifices of conflict, rendered ever greater by science and technology, have yielded very little indeed to the inviting prospects of cooperation.

Notes

1. See *The Current Digest of the Soviet Press*, vol. XXXV, no. 11 (13 April 1983).
2. For a stimulating reading of Lincoln's Second inaugral, see William Lee Miller, *A Study in Political Ethics*, available through the Poynter Center, Indiana University, Bloomington, Indiana 47401.
3. Takeshi Muramatsu, 'An Outline of the Japanese Way of Thinking', *Japan Report*,

vol. XXI, no. 6 (1 March 1975).
    4. *New York Times*, 15 July 1968.
    5. *New York Times*,   8 June 1972.

INDEX

114